TO OUR RESPECTIVE PARENTS...

# FROM HIGH SCHOOL TO MED. SCHOOL

1130-YANO

# FROM HIGH SCHOOL TO MED. SCHOOL

Jason Yanofski and
Ashish Raju

# ACKNOWLEDGEMENTS

We would like to thank the following people:

Drs. Balamurali "the world's youngest doctor" & Jayakrishna Ambati for providing us with the foreword and chapter eighteen. You were able to produce incredible work on short notice and have been supportive throughout. We thank you for taking time out of your busy schedules.

Dr. Judith Lasker for your essay about "medicine and society." We thank you for providing us with your expertise, contacts, and advice on our project, and we are grateful you could be a part of it.

Alexander Mitman for producing all the fantastic illustrations within this book. They really capture the essence of our message, and we feel fortunate to have been graced by your artistic talents. They make the book alive, and we never doubted that you were the best person for the job. Hopefully, we can work together again in the future.

Nihar Desai for the financial chapter. It is brilliant, and we predicted nothing less from you. You have surpassed our expectations as usual. Just as you've helped us with this book, we know that you have big things in your future, and we hope we can be a part of that one day.

Jamie Swanson for your behind the scenes interview and essay on double-majoring. You've been helpful from the very beginning to the final stages of editing, and we know our book is significantly better because of your special touch.

Anil Trindade for providing us with information about applying out of the program. You truly are the "real deal," and we wish you the best of luck in the future, wherever it may take you.

Hayley Teich for donating your application essay and your time in editing. This book would have many a typo if it wasn't for your help your help. We'll be sure to find you when we are ready to put out the second edition.

Dr. David Reibstein for submitting information on summer programs. Students, professors, and doctors who gave anecdotes or advice, teachers who provided sample recommendations, and everyone from Lehigh University and the West Orange crew (Mark, Will, Sasha, Tom, Maria, Dino, Oren, Rudy, Tina, Shuchi, Menka, and everyone who contributed in any way).

All the universities, medical schools, and organizations that responded to our surveys and provided us information through interviews, etc. AAMC for the statistics in their *MSAR* book, and *Academic Medicine* for permission to reprint from their journal.

Our respective families, especially our parents (to whom we dedicated this book) for continued support since the very beginning of this project. Thanks for generously helping by doing any and all of what was asked of you, including making phone calls and helping with tedious paperwork – and smiling the whole time. Most importantly, thanks for putting up with us.

Xlibris for all your services and guidance throughout the publication process.

THANKS EVERYONE!

# FOREWORD

## Drs. Balamurali K. Ambati & Jayakrishna Ambati

Albert Einstein once remarked about physicians, "There is no nobler endeavor in life than the assuaging of human suffering." It is refreshing and reassuring to see that despite all the turmoil that besets American medicine today, tomorrow's physicians still possess the requisite enthusiasm and dedication to renew our health care system. This book is an exquisite example.

There are many pathways to become a doctor. Many of our closest friends decided to pursue medicine in their 30s, after already being established in 1 or 2 other careers. We chose the short route: Jay graduated from medical school at 23 while Bala became the world's youngest doctor at 17. Neither of us went through a combined, accelerated BA/MD program, the subject of this book, but many of the challenges described herein are familiar. The authors are to be congratulated on the quality and applicability of their endeavor. They have chosen a topic that is relevant to a great number of high school students, and treated it with detail and brevity, candor and tact, and above all, clarity.

This book marshals information that is hard-to-find but invaluable to the prospective applicant, as parents, teachers, and guidance counselors are all too often ignorant of this promising career option. Further, from this compendium they have culled advice that will point many a student in the right direction. Throughout they have struck the right balance of authority and informality to inform and engage the reader.

Training to be a doctor is a long and stressful road. This book lights a shorter path and eases much of the stress. It should become the standard of its class, and be read by any high school student considering a career in medicine.

Balamurali K. Ambati, MD
Jayakrishna Ambati, MD

# CONTENTS

# PREFACE

Getting into medical school is a goal pursued by many, but only realized by a few. For four years of college, supposedly the best years of your life, you are putting all your eggs in one basket. You are working harder than you've ever worked before, just for a chance of getting accepted into medical school, so that you can work even harder. There must be another way—and there is. "Get with the program!"

We are referring to programs currently available in which high school students apply for a guaranteed acceptance to medical school based on their high school performance. Not only is their future guaranteed, but their undergraduate years are shortened too. These six and seven-year accelerated medical programs are the fastest, cheapest, and easiest way to get into medical school.

What is unfortunate is that hardly anyone understands what the programs are, despite the fact that more people are applying every year. This book will explain the advantages and disadvantages of participating in such programs, what it takes to get accepted, the steps of the process, and all the issues encountered throughout. Not only that, but quotes taken from interviews with high school, college, and medical school students and advisors, doctors, and organizations will give you a complete spread of opinions about all aspects of the program.

The first chapter is designed to introduce you to accelerated medical programs and what they are all about. The second chapter examines the pros and cons to help you decide if they are right for you. Chapter Three will give you an overview of what the competition is like and show you where you stand. The next two chapters will help you succeed in high school (academically and outside of the classroom). You'll learn what kinds of activities you will want to be involved in (during the school year and during the summer) to maximize your chances of being accepted into a program.

Chapters Six through Nine are designed to help you along the entire application process. You'll learn how to fill out your forms, write your personal statement, acquire effective letters of recommendation, and prepare for interviews. You will also see the relative importance of each of these steps.

In Chapter Ten, we'll tell you how to handle rejection and acceptance. Chapter Eleven will get you ready for college, and Chapter Twelve will help you handle your finances. Chapter Thirteen will answer your questions about the curriculum and interacting with professors and your advisor. In the fourteenth chapter, we'll help you to become effective at studying so you can stay at the top of your game.

Chapter Fifteen will guide you through the rest of college life, outside of the classroom, and Chapter Sixteen will tell you how to deal with the Medical College Admissions Test. Chapter Seventeen will help in the transition from college to medical school. It will also address such issues as quitting the program and being released.

Chapter Eighteen will tell you about the life of a medical school student and what you will face later on in the field. In Chapter Nineteen, we'll tell you about other accelerated programs within the health field and programs that allow you to combine your medical degree with another graduate degree. Finally, Chapter Twenty provides a look at what the field of medicine will be like in the upcoming years and a short conclusion to the book.

For reference purposes, Appendix A contains information about each of the programs nationwide and the *only* system of ranking currently in existence for medical programs. Appendix B has a journal article and research abstracts examining how accelerated students fare relative to traditional medical students and whether or not the purposes of accelerated programs are being met. In Appendix C, you'll find additional information about summer programs, and Appendix D provides useful web sites by category.

At the end of the book, you can find out how to get in touch with us to ask questions or to submit ideas for our next edition. You can also find information about the authors in a section creatively titled, "About the Authors." If after reading the book, you still crave more knowledge about accelerated medical programs, make sure to stop by our web page (www.AcceleratedMed.com) for an interactive, educational experience.

We hope that this book will help acquaint students with a serious interest in medicine to the possibilities offered by accelerated medical programs. From our personal experience and hardships in discovering all the intricacies of accelerated programs, we have been able to incorporate our thoughts, ideas, and advice along with those of fellow peers and professionals to aid you, the student, in your journey.

This book aims to encompass and develop the academic, social, and psychological aspects of the college application process from the angle of accelerated medical programs. Many of our own conventions and quirks can be seen within its chapters, and hopefully we've provided a more personal approach to what could otherwise have been another mundane "how-to" book.

Also, it was our style choice to pick pronouns to represent specific groups and utilize them whenever relevant, as opposed to a "him or her" convention. We *do* recognize that half the accelerated students are females, etc. In summation, we hope you find this book informative, fun to read and most importantly, an invaluable resource in your life.

# UNIT I

*Get with the program!*

# CHAPTER 1

## Accelerated Medical Huh?

*"Today, if you are not confused, you are just*
*not thinking clearly."*
—U. Peter

*"Try to find your deepest issue in every*
*confusion, and abide by that."*
—D. H. Lawrence

This chapter is a general overview of accelerated medical programs and contains many references to other chapters where more information on specific topics can be found.

## So what exactly is a guaranteed accelerated medical program?

Accelerated medical programs are programs where qualified students can gain a conditional acceptance to medical school directly from high school. With the difficulty of attaining a medical school position in recent years, many high school students have decided to pursue this alternative route.

The accelerated programs provide a condensed track through college of only two or three years. After this time, as long as the student has met all requirements placed on him by the program (See Chapter 6), he will matriculate to the medical school. There are also many programs that guarantee your medical school position after four years of college. Though these programs aren't accelerated, they *do* provide many of the same advantages as six and seven-year programs.

## Terminology

The programs in this book go by several names. The terms **BA/MD program** and **guaranteed medical program** both refer to the idea that conditional medical school acceptance is in conjunction with the college acceptance. The terms **accelerated medical program**, **combined medical program**, and **6-year** or **7-year medical program** recognize the quick pace. However, all of these terms refer to the same type of program. This doesn't mean that there aren't inherent differences between different programs nationwide, as you will see in the next chapter.

When doing comparisons, we are going to refer to non-program students as traditional students or **traditionals**. Students who are participating in a program will be called program students or **programmers**.

## What are the differences between programs?

There are many differences between programs, and information on each program can be found in the back of this book. Some of these differences will help you decide which programs are more suited for you. (See Chapter 2)

### Medical school location

By medical school location, we mean relative to the university where you receive your undergraduate education. Some medical schools may be on the same campus as the undergraduate institution. Thus, the medical school is directly affiliated with the college and most likely they share the same name. This means that you will be in the same place for all six, seven, or eight years.

On the other hand, the medical school may be in another city altogether. These schools are not directly affiliated with the under-graduate institutions. Instead, they agree ahead of time to accept students from the universities on certain conditions.

**Length of time**
Length of time refers to the number of years spent in college. Medical school is always four years and cannot be accelerated. Seven-year programs require three years in college, and six-year programs require only two (and probably one summer). Some programs will allow a choice between two or three years. Non-accelerated eight-year programs usually parallel a traditional pre-med curriculum.

The trend over the last few years has been to move away from the short six-year programs because it is felt by many that these programs do not make for good doctors, despite research that shows otherwise. (See Appendix B) For example, the Union College program recently changed its seven-year program into an eight-year program.

Number of current accelerated programs by length:

- 3 six-year programs
- 13 seven-year programs
- 5 six/seven-year programs
- 3 seven to nine-year programs
- 14 eight-year programs

**MCAT**
The Medical College Admissions Test (MCAT) is a very important test for traditionals. Programmers can tackle this test with a slightly different mindset. Some programs do not require students to take the test. Others do require the test, but they may have no required scores that need to be obtained. In this sense, the test is just a formality. The third option is that specific MCAT scores need to be attained before the student is able to move on to medical school.

The student will usually get multiple opportunities to take it. (See Chapter 17)

### GPA requirement

All programs will have some grade point average (GPA) requirement that must be maintained in order to move on to the medical school. Some programs require that a separate science and overall GPA be looked at, but other ones value only the overall GPA. Generally, the necessary GPA is equivalent to around a B+, but this may vary greatly.

### Major and course requirements

Your curriculum will vary depending upon where you are. For example, at the Lehigh University accelerated program, programmers will have pre-medical sciences as their major, a major not offered to anyone else at the school. In this case, traditional premeds will have to choose a "real" major in addition to taking all the necessary pre-medical courses. On the other hand, at some schools programmers are required to double-major or may have special commitments added to their curriculum.

It is also important to note that the rules often change. A student in Brooklyn College's BA/MD program told us:

> Many of the rules and requirements for the program dramatically changed the year after my entering year. From what I hear of the new requirements, I would think that the program is much harder and much less flexible than when I entered. I'm not even sure that I would want to be in it with the way it is now for incoming students.

### College and medical school differences

The colleges and medical schools themselves will have many differences. Colleges can be big or small, state schools or private schools, and in big cities or in the middle of nowhere. Some may be more generous with scholarships than others, and every school will have its own subtle nuances that make it unique. The differences are countless, and you will want to visit them and talk to people. Our profiles section will be able to help you, as well.

Medical schools are no less different, and often they are geared towards specific specialties. A major difference between medical schools is whether they are **allopathic** or **osteopathic**. Osteopathic schools are generally less competitive and have somewhat different curricula. They tend to have a philosophy of treating the patient more as a whole as opposed to focusing on specific parts. One osteopathic doctor told us, "Our training is the same. We have the same exact books, but we spend more time on anatomy and physiology. Structure and function."

Medical schools also may be ranked differently relative to each other, and this might be something to consider when trying to obtain a competitive residency. For more information about specific medical schools you may want to look at a book called *Medical School Admission Requirements* (*MSAR*) published each year by the American Association of Medical Colleges (AAMC).

**Other**
There are special characteristics or requirements that are unique to certain programs. Flexibility of such things as class selection and electives vary. You may or may not be able to take pass/fail courses, transfer credits from another university, etc. Also, certain programs may be especially geared towards minorities or residents of a particular state or region. For example, the University of Illinois at Chicago program only allows students from Illinois to apply.

Appendix A has programs ranked in different categories, but you will want to seek out more information on your own before you can decide which program is right for you.

## Sounds competitive

Getting into an accelerated medical program is extremely competitive. Acceptance rates of medical programs challenge those of

Ivy League schools. (See Chapter 3) Many candidates are extremely qualified. But don't worry, we'll show you what it takes to get into an accelerated medical program in the following chapters.

**Will *I* be accepted?**
Stranger things *have* happened. Keep on reading!

**If thousands of people apply and there are less than twenty people in the program each year, how can I expect to have a chance at being accepted?**
Don't get scared by numbers. Looking at statistics of how many people are in a program at a certain school will not necessarily represent the number of students that were accepted. Many applicants may have opted not to take the program route. Others may have multiple acceptances and attend the one of their choice.

In many years, the same batch of students is applying to these programs, and you are solely competing against each other. The total number of applications to all the programs may be even more misleading if you consider that one student may apply to ten or more programs.

## Some history

Combined BA/MD programs first came into existence in the early 1960s. They have gone through changes since then. There have also been studies since the beginning, monitoring the effectiveness and ramifications of such programs. (See Appendix B)

## Let me get this straight (Q&A)

**Am I really applying for medical school while I'm in high school?**
Yes, you are applying for a conditional acceptance to medical school from high school. The interview will take place at the medical school. They are the ones who will be looking over your application and making the final decision. Most of the elements necessary

for the traditional medical school application are still there, but you are judged on the fact that you are a high school student with the ability to become a qualified doctor in time.

### So if I make a program I won't need to go through the medical school application at all?

You will have to apply to medical school. However, this is once again a formality. Unlike thousands of other applicants, you have already been conditionally accepted and are going through "the motions" of the application process. You will still have to fill out the AMCAS application, medical school forms, and prepare a résumé. Even though you have an acceptance, you should still be wary of clauses in your contract that will allow the medical school to release you under certain conditions. (See Chapter 17)

### Why do these programs even exist?

Good question. These programs are generally designed for medical schools to attract over-achieving students early on. Some programs also have other goals in mind. They may try to push students to work in poor areas later on or in underrepresented fields.

### How is it even possible to complete four years of college in two or three years?

That isn't really what's going on. Traditional students spend much time exploring their options during their college years. Since you already know that you want to become a doctor, you can take the specific pre-requisites medical schools are looking for in two to three years.

The remaining credits needed for graduation are then transferred back from your first year of medical school. If this is the case for your specific program, you won't get your college diploma until you complete your first year in medical school.

### Why can't I find any general information about these programs?

The existence of accelerated medical programs isn't a secret. Yet, many people who could benefit from them aren't aware of their availability. It seems that the only way people know about these programs is through friends who are or were in them

One student told us, "I explored other BA/MD programs through the college office . . . but there was no good or comprehensive source that covered all programs." This opinion was not unique. Here is what we found to be a typical conversation with high school guidance counselors:

**AcceleratedMed:**
What advice would you give to students interested in accelerated medical programs? I am referring to BA/MD programs, in which high school students are accepted into medical school under a conditional guarantee. Are you familiar with such programs?
**Counselor:**
I hate to sound ignorant, but I was not aware of that being available. We have had no students participate in such a program during my time as a counselor.
**AcceleratedMed:**
Don't you think that this could be attributed to the lack of knowledge? If you were not aware of the existence of these programs, then why would you expect your students to be? Isn't it your job to find out about such things and to let them know?
**Counselor:**
Yes, but only if the information related to new programs at the various universities is given to the counselors. However, it sounds like an excellent idea—tell me more!
**AcceleratedMed:**
These programs are offered through more than 40 participating universities with affiliations through either their medical schools or another medical school. Some of the contingencies of their medical school spot include GPA and MCAT requirements.
**Counselor:**
That sounds like an excellent plan—I wonder why I've never received any info on it. Are any of the schools in Ohio?

**AcceleratedMed:**
Yes, Case Western Reserve University has one, and there are many others in Ohio and nearby states.

**Counselor:**
Well, now that I know it exists, I will definitely let my students know about this option!

**AcceleratedMed:**
Why do you think many guidance counselors do not know about these prestigious programs that are as competitive as the Ivy Leagues? Don't you think that there are a lot of students missing out on chances because of this lack of knowledge?

**Counselor:**
Absolutely—the schools that offer the programs should be more aggressive in their advertisements.

**AcceleratedMed:**
Hopefully our book would shed more light on this subject.

Now that you have read this far and learned that there is a way to guarantee your future, you must be relieved. Feel free to contact us to express how lost you would have been if we hadn't enlightened you. Actually, let's see if you get in first! You still have a long way to go in the application process as well as nineteen more chapters . . . Read on!

# CHAPTER 2

## The Program and You

*"It is not in the stars to hold our destiny but in ourselves."*
—William Shakespeare

*"Don't be afraid to take a big step. You can't
cross a chasm in two small jumps."*
—David Lloyd George

Now that you know what accelerated programs are about, you probably have a general feeling of whether or not you would have an interest in participating. This chapter will help you decide if you should apply.

## Medicine as a career

It is probably the case that you are very interested in attending medical school if you are reading this book. However, it is important that you really understand what you are getting yourself into. Medicine is a big commitment, and medical school is difficult! But medicine can also be rewarding, as well as lucrative. It will allow you to help others and be respected.

For more information about what medical school is like and what you will face afterwards, see Chapters 18 and 20. This book, however, is not the forum to decide whether medicine is for you. You really should talk to a lot of doctors and others in the field to see what they have to say. It takes a very mature high school mind to know whether a career in medicine is right for them.

Going pre-med traditionally may seem like a similar commitment since the program can usually be dropped pretty easily, but four years at college will allow more time for exploration of different fields of study, as well as more opportunities to do internships and research in the medical field. It would be a shame to make it all the way to medical school before you found out that you couldn't stand the sight of blood. These are some characteristics that are important to posses as physician:

- Commitment
- Passion for learning
- Not afraid of challenges
- Endurance
- Intelligence
- Organization
- Enjoy helping people
- Patience (no pun intended)

## Traditional vs. accelerated

If you are confident that medical school is for you, being accepted to an accelerated medical program can be a great opportunity. There are many bitter traditionals that wish they could turn back the clock and go the program route. On the other hand, there are much fewer program alumni who regret the choices *they've* made. But even so, accelerated programs are not for everyone. This chapter will help you decide if programs are right for *you*.

## Advantages of the accelerated route

Why do so many students apply to programs? There are obviously many benefits, and this section will guide you through them.

### Guaranteed acceptance

By participating in an accelerated program, you will not have the stress that normally comes with the territory of being a traditional pre-med. They'll sweat through every minute of it, and even the strongest applicants will bite their fingernails as they wait by the mailbox to find out which schools they've made—if any. It is definitely nice to have security. With your relaxed atmosphere, maybe you can even have a social life and do other college type stuff! (See Chapter 15)

### Specified requirements

A traditional student never really knows where they stand. Programmers, however, always know how they are doing. A clear-cut GPA requirement allows students to relax when they're in good standing. Clearly defined Medical College Admissions Test (MCAT) scores make it easy to decide whether or not it is necessary to retest. The MCAT is essentially turned into a pass-fail exam. (See Chapter 16)

### Nobody to impress

Traditional students have much résumé-building to do. To even have a chance at medical school, they'll need to participate in activities like volunteer work, internships, and research. Programmers have the option of spending their time in these ways, but they are not obligated to do so. If they choose to, it's their prerogative.

This same principle applies to course selection. How about taking a double-major? (See Chapter 13) Or perhaps you'd rather just take a light semester and party every night—before you get to the hard stuff. Individual program workloads and commitments will vary, and it is best to contact students in the programs to find out such inside information.

### Accelerated route

Many people feel that four years of college is too long. Their opinion is that while it is an important time for personal growth, not all individuals require that many years of academic and social development. They have another four years of medical school ahead of them, not including residency time and fellowship. Every year saved definitely helps in the larger picture. If you crave a more rigorous schedule and really want to learn at a fast pace, then accelerated programs provide this important advantage for you.

### Save money

Financially, avoiding a year or two of college can make a big difference and amount to thousands of saved dollars. However, saving money should not be the prime impetus for pursuing a medical program. Most medical students have huge debts, and two years of college tuition will not matter in the long run when you are practicing medicine. Time is money, but money cannot buy back time.

Make sure that you are factoring in that state colleges and state medical schools are cheaper than private schools. Also, be aware that participating in the program may disqualify you from certain scholarships and/or grants in medical school. (See Chapter 12)

### No need to apply

Traditional pre-meds have to jump through several hoops for medical school admissions. Personal statements, résumés, and recommendations from professors are just the beginning. Generally, program students will have to go through similar things before entering the medical school, but only as formalities. (See Chapter 17)

### Prestige

It's nice to leave high school with a conditional medical school acceptance under your belt. Yale who? This is great for bragging, if you're into that sort of thing. However, there are always two sides to every issue, as you will see later on. Ah, what the heck. We'll just tell you right now!

# All right already, what about the disadvantages?

Because you can usually be released from programs if you want to leave, there aren't really many disadvantages in participation. Of course, changing your major may mean that all the science courses you've taken could have been a waste of time, and you may switch from being accelerated to being behind.

**Missed opportunities**
If you do go to a university because of a program and later decide that you don't want to be in it, you may be in a school that isn't as perfect for you as another that you passed up. Choosing between a program and an Ivy League school may be a difficult decision, but hopefully not one that you will regret.

There are, of course, very prestigious programs such as Brown, Northwestern, Rice, Penn State, Lehigh, etc. (See Appendix A) These programs are extremely competitive, though. Acceptance into a program obviously means acceptance into the participating university, but it is possible to be accepted into the university but not the program. Because of this, it is reasonable to think that someone who has been accepted into programs has also been accepted into universities ranked higher than the schools affiliated with the programs that they made—Did you catch all that?! For this reason, it is likely that you will have the need to take an important introspective look at what's really important to you, school reputation or assurance of a medical degree. The following college sophomore shares the decision that she made:

> *Throughout high school, I had been sure of what I wanted to ultimately become: a physician. When I applied to Johns Hopkins and subsequently was accepted, I figured that I was on my way. My first semester, I took the standard pre-med courses and throughout the year followed a rigorous schedule in a highly competitive environment, which I had expected. The one thing that I didn't expect was to change my mind.*

*Halfway through my second semester of my freshman year,
I came to the realization that pre-med was not something I
wanted to do; instead I found that economics was something
that interested me immensely. Though I could have chosen an
accelerated program, I left my options open so that I could be
certain that I had picked a major that I really wanted. Though
I do not regret the decision I have made, I do know that if I was
at an accelerated pre-med program, I may not have had the
freedom to make such a choice, and might have ended up feeling
restricted to doing something that didn't fully appeal to me.*

*Constantine Konstantakis*

## Locked into one medical school?

If you want to apply to other schools, you will almost always need
to quit the program, and then you take the risk of not being accepted anywhere. So, unless you are fairly confident that your application is strong enough to impress your dream school, it may
not be a good idea to take that chance. This may also be a very
tough decision, and the prestige factor again comes into play. (See
Chapter 17)

## Lost college years

College is said by many to be the best years of your life. However,
some will say that you really can't participate in everything if you
are only there for 2-3 years. An accelerated program does cut down
your college experience, and that is something you must consider
especially if you are unsure about your career goals.

At the same time, being in a program may allow you to be
more flexible and to do things that traditionals do not have the
chance to experience. They may be too busy trying to maintain a
pristine college record for medical school admission. You should
also consider whether you want more years in college, or more
years in your profession.

*Through my program, I only went to college for two years,
and I may have regretted doing so if I had to spend that time
like the non-program students did, working non-stop. Because
of my more relaxed environment, I had an active social life. I
really feel that my two years were very dense, and I have no
regrets because I experienced a lot.*

*Jason Yanofski*

## Who are these programs for?

These programs are designed for students who want to become
doctors, have performed exceptionally in high school, and value
security over prestige. One student told us:

*Being in a program, you can get away with a less aca-
demically impressive record than someone trying to get into
med. school traditionally. This also allows you room to take a lot
of classes of your choice. I'm taking a lot of fun classes, and I have
time to do other things because I don't have to worry about
getting A's in everything.*

*Judith Flom*

Here, a program student tells us what she's learned about the
type of students who attend accelerated programs:

*I can vividly recall the day that I interviewed for medical
school. I had only applied to one accelerated program, as a fluke.
I originally had intended to become a biomedical engineer.*

*On the day I walked into the admissions office, I really
thought I had made a mistake. I stood there, decked out in my
short plaid skirt with a purple pinstripe shirt. Everyone else was
in suits, or at least conservative colors. I swore that I felt their eyes
roll with every turn of my shiny highlighted hair, but I mustered
up some courage and decided to have a good time. It might be the
only time I ever set foot inside a medical school, I thought. So I*

*cracked jokes on the tour. I argued with my interviewer. My mother even inadvertently insulted the other students' parents because she pretended she did not know what an AP credit was.*

*But months later I received an acceptance letter. Maybe the BA/MD programs weren't just for nerds, I thought. I had the same grades and SAT. I was involved in plenty of extracurricular activities. I certainly believe that I have the "people" skills necessary to be a doctor. That's when I realized that my stereotype of students who applied to accelerated programs, and pre-meds in general, was wrong.*

*Now I believe that students who enter accelerated pre-medical programs usually come in two types. The first type is still the stereotypical "nerd." These students are the ones who have researched the medical school before the interview. They carry briefcases and take as many honors classes as they possibly can. He or she has a singular goal in life—to become a doctor in as little amount of time as possible. The program is designed perfectly for students like these. They only have to take the required classes in as little as two years, and they will be doctors at the age of 24. They are definitely the type of people I would trust in an operating room, but they are usually not the most fun-loving crowd.*

*However, accelerated programs also attract another type of student, the highly ambitious and creative type. They might not fit the traditional model of a pre-med, but they can be just as successful as doctors. These students usually choose to stay three or four years. The extra year or two of college can give students the chance to work on a second major, study abroad, hold an office in student senate, pledge a fraternity or sorority, or simply "experience college."*

*Jamie Swanson*

## Myths about programs

The purpose of this book is not to convince students to take an accelerated route. We are merely providing the information necessary to make an informed decision. That in mind, we hope to provide you with an objective perspective. We do find it our job, however, to respond to the rationalizations made by traditional students and adversaries to accelerated programs. The fact is that many of them are jealous, and we would be too.

Most traditional students who have graduated from medical schools look down upon programs as unfair loopholes with bad consequences. They believe that these programs are an injustice to the medical profession. In reality, they did not go through a program, and they know very little about them. If you had gone through eight years of schooling, without a guarantee to obtain your degree, and then found out that a program existed in which you could have attained that same degree in six years, you would be a little peeved too. We are writing this book to spread objective information so that the aforementioned hypothetical will never occur.

In the mean time, though, accelerated medical degree programs have received quite a bit of scrutiny by several individuals. Professors, students, and doctors often have strong opinions one way or the other without really knowing the facts, and many writers of 'how-to' books concerning medical school admissions have also put in their two cents. The following is a list of common misconceptions.

**"They are impossible to get into."**
First of all, these programs are highly competitive. There is no doubt about that. Some programs have thousands of students applying for less than 30 seats. You can do the math on that one. However, if you are afraid of competition, medicine probably isn't the field for you anyway.

Individuals who are rejected would like to think that nobody gets in. However, it is more likely that the real reason they weren't accepted is that they lacked the passion, academics, or personality to get into medical school. It is also a possibility that they were perfect candidates who did not get in because medical schools simply cannot absorb everyone who is qualified and motivated. (See Chapter 3)

**"They are highly intense."**
This is not necessarily true. College is intense in general, especially pre-med. Accelerated programs are within the confines of college, and most program students take classes with other non-program students. Generally, the curriculum consists of the classes that are required for medical school and many electives as well. This varies, of course, from school to school.

Some people think that a six-year program crams all of four years of college into two years. If that were the case, it would be a miracle if anyone survived, and the exaggeration exists because many people are not familiar with how the programs work. The acceleration is possible by having certain credits count toward both college and medical school degrees simultaneously. If we thought that eight years of schooling was being reduced to six, we'd cringe too.

**"You don't learn everything you need to become a good doctor."**
Even though there are mixed opinions regarding whether accelerated students are mature enough to become doctors, research has consistently shown that they *do* excel relative to traditional students later in life. (See Appendix B) Here, one student speaks his mind:

> *Although I am applying to cooperative medical programs at several undergraduate institutions with 8-year programs (Siena College and University of Rochester), I have a mixed opinion on 6-year accelerated programs. It seems to me that treating patients is an important responsibility that requires a*

*certain level of maturity as well as a certain amount of book training. Regardless of how much more "crunched" these programs are in terms of their course load, its graduates will still be two years younger than the rest of their peers and at a certain disadvantage in maturity levels. I'm not saying it these doctors can't be good ones, but if I'm in the hospital as a patient, I think I'd appreciate to be treated by a more experienced physician (experienced in life in general as well as science).*

The truth of the matter is that no medical school would allow unqualified students to graduate as doctors. Once again, a shortened program does not mean that you leave out vital parts of the curricula. Most non-program students spend a lot of time in college taking courses that are not involved with their final major or profession at all. They use this period to discover what they want to be. If you graduate from high school and know that medicine is your calling, then this time spent in college is not advantageous. That is why you can attend a 6 or 7-year medical program without missing out. You still learn everything that the traditional student learns.

If you know for sure that you want to be a doctor, why should you spend extra years in school, take classes that are not suited for you, and undergo unwarranted stress? People falsely assume that medical program graduates cut corners and take the minimum amount of work. However, the shortening occurs in the undergraduate years, not the four years of medical school. Thus, the specialized skills needed to become a doctor are learned in medical school whether or not you're a program student. For all you know, your *own* doctor may have even graduated from a program!

### "You are losing 1-2 of the best years of your life."
You might have heard that college is the best time of your life. However, for students wishing to become doctors, college can become a nightmare. Traditional medical school applicants hide themselves in libraries memorizing facts upon facts. They cry over missed

points on exams and their hurt GPA. They have anxiety over whether they will get into medical school. Extra curricular activities stretch these students thin and wear them out. Honestly, is this really the best time of your life?

While in a program, you know what is expected of you in terms of GPA and MCAT scores. There is no need to be so competitive and filled with angst. You are conditionally accepted to medical school. You will see that program students usually have a better college experience than traditional medical school applicants do because they can always keep things in perspective.

**"Students who pursue accelerated medical programs are the ones who can't get into medical school traditionally."**
This is very far from the truth. The admissions rates for accelerated and combined degree programs rival those of Ivy League schools. Students that are accepted into medical programs are very intelligent, mature, and know that they want to pursue medicine as a career. Studies have shown that students who are accepted by accelerated programs generally are as successful (if not more successful) than traditional students. Again, see the research in Appendix B.

## Q&A

**I have been accepted to an accelerated medical degree program and an Ivy League school. Where should I go?**
More often than not, this is a problem that many students applying to accelerated degree programs face. Your friends may mock you for going to a no-name school. You might feel bad giving up crimson colors, settling for something less, but when you look at the whole picture, you'll realize that you aren't settling at all.

It is just as difficult and at times even more difficult to gain entrance to medical degree programs. There is no "guarantee" that you will make it into medical school if you pursue the traditional route, even if you go to a prestigious undergraduate school. If you are mature enough and know for sure that you want to be a physician, why wait and risk it?

After you graduate from medical school, your undergraduate education is trivial. It may feel nice to say, "I graduated from Harvard University." However, that's all it is, a name, and it doesn't come with a medical degree. Competition exists for medical school after four years of college as well as after your senior year in high school. The question you must ask yourself is, "Where do I stand the best chance of getting in?" You can decide where to go based on that answer.

*I very much enjoyed my time at the BU program and would recommend the program to anyone who is sure that they want to be a physician. If you aren't sure, you're better off waiting to finish college, as this is a big decision.*

Elaine Melamud, M.D.

**Is admission to medical school traditionally really that competitive?**
In a word, yes! Medical school admissions are extremely competitive and justifiably so. We wouldn't want our doctors to be incompetent. If a mechanic makes a mistake, you can always fix the car. However, a doctor doesn't have that luxury. There are always far more applications to medical school than available seats. A recent estimate is that for every seat there are 3-4 qualified applicants. This is the reason why many students are now seeking entrance to medical school via accelerated medical degree programs.

# CHAPTER 3

## The Competition

*"And while the law [of competition] may be sometimes hard
for the individual, it is best for the race, because it ensures the
survival of the fittest in every department."*
—Andrew Carnegie

*"Shoot for the moon. Even if you miss,
you'll land among the stars."*
—Les Brown

Now that you know what accelerated medical programs are about
and that you want to apply, this chapter will give you a feeling of
where you stand. You'll get to see what the application numbers
are like and what kinds of applicants admissions is looking to accept.

The following chapters will delineate specific aspects of the
application process in more detail. The first part of this chapter is
an overview of the competition. Make sure to see our stats later in
this chapter. It is there that you will see the real math behind the
numbers.

## Application requirements

When applying to programs, there are usually two requirements
that must be met before admissions will even view your application. The first is that you be ranked within a certain percentage of

your class (approximately top five or ten percent). The second requirement is that you reach a specific Standardized Aptitude Test (SAT) score, which could be anywhere from 1300 to 1500. To apply to the Penn State program, for example, students must be in the top tenth of the class and have received at least a 1440 on their SAT. You may take the SAT as many times as you want, but you cannot add verbal and math section scores from different tests. Each program may also have additional requirements and inherent eccentricities.

## What do I need to do to get in?!

Chill out . . . We'll help you get through this. You don't need to be a genius to be accepted into the program. You just need to be generally impressive and competitive among the other applicants. As long as you have met the applications requirements and have a résumé that proves that you can handle the accelerated course load, you are definitely in the race.

Killer SAT scores and valedictory status are a plus, but it is more important to be able to show that you can balance your time and work hard. The key is being diversified. While some admissions committees will stress certain factors over others, there is a basic formula that you should follow, and this formula will be crystal clear by the end of Chapter 5. To give you a taste of what's to come, here is what one student told us:

> Make sure you have a well-rounded application . . . I have friends who earned higher grade point averages than mine, but they didn't play any instruments, and they didn't have as eclectic of a résumé. So my advice is to join teams and clubs in an effort to explore non-science interests. But don't let your grades suffer.

## Applying to med. programs vs. colleges

No matter where you apply, if it's competitive, you will need to have impressive academics. For programs, this is especially important, and there are *no* exceptions. Traditional colleges may trade off stellar grades for exceptional sports or music, but programs are not as lenient. They have a lot at stake if you can't handle your academics, and so they justifiably demand a lot from their applicants.

Colleges use SAT scores and class rank as subjective guidelines. Programs do this to a certain extent, but there are very strict standards on the lower end. As you will find out later in this chapter, these standards are such that if your score is below a certain point, your application will be tossed aside without further reading. The competitiveness of particular schools can be seen in Appendix A.

Universities will also look at extracurricular activities. Programs, however, have more specific tastes, and getting involved and obtaining leadership positions with certain activities will pay off big time. These areas include volunteer work, research, and medical experience. (See Chapter 5)

Some parts of the application are objective (your SAT score), but other parts are *subjective* (extracurricular activities). The subjective parts may make some applicants more attractive to some programs than others. It can even come down to the specific interviewer that you have. They may feel that students who work after school are very responsible. Someone else will be impressed with research accomplishments or think that leadership experience is the most important thing. An applicant may be immediately rejected when it is seen that they have no experience in the field of medicine.

While chapter five will provide a general formula for you to follow, it is hard to find out exactly what formula is necessary to increase your chances at a *specific* program, especially since this changes yearly. Talking to students can help, but there is never a guarantee, and so your best bet is to try to cover all your bases.

## Example profiles

At this stage in the game, you're probably thinking, "I wish I had some example profiles of candidates that did and did not make good impressions upon admissions." Raise your hand if that is what you're thinking. We don't see any hands. Oh wait, there's one guy in the back – or is he just scratching his head? Well, even if we help only one person, it'll be worthwhile in our minds. So, here you go!

**Candidate A (Friar Tuck):**
SAT 1240, Top 25%, president of the French club, good recommendations.

This applicant shouldn't plan on receiving acceptances from programs any time soon. Not only are his academics poor, but his résumé is very skimpy. Unfortunately for him, nothing he has to offer even warrants a second look.

**Candidate B (Yoda):**
SAT 1450, Top 1%, many AP classes, vice-president of the ecology club, positions in other high school clubs, active in church, volunteered at hospital during senior year, good personal statement.

This applicant is strong enough academically, but not impressive otherwise. School clubs can only take you so far, and a stronger leadership role would help a lot here. His other activities seem weak. An exceptional essay and glowing recommendation may afford him a chance.

**Candidate C (Flint):**
SAT 1320, Top 15%, some AP classes, some SAT II tests, volunteers with a surgeon multiple times a week, president of student council, president of National Honor Society, editor of school paper, many awards, research experience for two summers, excellent recommendations.

This applicant has impressive achievements, however his academics are relatively low. He will have difficulty passing requirements necessary even to apply, and will have a harder time getting in. However, his recommendations and strong leadership roles will keep him in the race if his SAT score can be bumped up another 100 points. He may consider taking a test prep course.

**Candidate D (Bilbo Baggins):**
SAT 1400, Top 4%, several AP classes, good SAT II tests, volunteer EMT, captain of first aid youth squad, prestigious research experience, leadership position in job, captain of wrestling team, some national awards, very strong recommendations.

This applicant has impressive academics and very strong activities. With a moving personal statement and good interview, he could make out very well.

**Candidate E (Igor):**
SAT 1600, valedictorian, received a score of 5 on every AP test in existence, Olympic swimmer, runner and weightlifter, did research and discovered a cure for cancer, internship with the surgeon general, mayor of his town, recommendation from the Pope and the President, published a "how-to" book about getting into accelerated medical programs.

This applicant would never exist. They would get in anywhere, but they should still apply to some back-up programs just in case!

## Our own number crunching statistics

**Medical School Admission Requirements, United States and Canada, 1999-2000 by Association of American Medical Colleges Staff and Kimberly S. Varner**

According to information in the AAMC's *MSAR*, in the 1997-1998 year, there were 43,020 medical school applicants who sent out 512,878 applications. This means each individual sent applications to an average of 11.9 schools. There were 16,165 enrollments that year, implying that 37.6% got in, which is about 1 out of 3. This refers only to those medical school hopefuls who actually sent in their applications. There were many others that started off college as a pre-med but never finished the curriculum, or didn't consider themselves with high enough credentials to apply. These people aren't factored in.

Of the applicants who were of 20 years or younger, the acceptance rate was 69.5 %, higher than any other category. This is also one of the smallest categories, making up only 1.7 percent of the total applicant pool. The high rate cannot be attributed to students who were going through programs because they were not included in this statistic. These are students who managed to finish college on their own in two years or who skipped grades in high school. Since age is supposedly not a factor that is looked at when determining admission to medical school, the youngest group must have had the highest scores. This is impressive, considering that they pushed themselves through at the fastest pace.

The number of applicants in that group was small at 719, but it is doubtful that it was an anomaly when it is seen that every increasing age group actually had lower acceptance rates than the group before it in a very linear fashion. The next age group, 21-23 (which was the largest, including more than half the total applicants), had only a 47.8% acceptance rate, and group after that had only 32.1%. The oldest group, including everyone 38 and older had an acceptance rate of 20.7%. The average age of all applicants was 24.6 and the average age of the applicants accepted was 23.9. These numbers imply that the best chance of getting in belongs to those who finish quickly and move on. There is less room for error that way, apparently.

19,124 applications were sent out to programs. Assuming that students applied to an average of five schools (which may not be accurate), then that would mean that there were about 4,000 applicants. 967 students attended programs in that year. Based on there being 44 programs, this makes an average of 22 students attending each individual program in that year (numbers in each program will fluctuate greatly).

This means that about 1 out of 4 students, or 25%, was accepted to at least one program, including 8-year programs, which are not accelerated and much less competitive, despite their guarantee. Many of the prestigious six and seven-year programs have lower acceptance rates, and students are already weeded out by the strict SAT and class rank requirements necessary even to apply.

The school with one of the lowest numbers of program students was Binghamton University with only 12 applicants, 11 of which were interviewed and 3 accepted. This is an 8-year program. On the other end of the spectrum is Brown University's 8-year program with 2,018 applicants and 55 accepted. Fisk University had even more applicants for its 8-year program. 5,453 applied and 80 were accepted. 6 and 7-year programs proved much more competitive, with typically a couple hundred applicants and only about fifteen acceptances per year, though this varied widely.

## Behind the scenes

Jamie Swanson, a journalism and pre-med double-major interviewed Maura Kugelman, assistant director of admissions for the Lehigh University accelerated program. Here is her report:

The process of initially weeding through applications takes place in the undergraduate admissions office. There, admissions officers recommend certain applicants to the medical schools for interviews.

The process does not differ much from standard college admissions, according to Maura J. Kugelman, Assistant Director of Admissions at Lehigh University.

Kugelman has worked as the liaison between Lehigh University and MCP-Hahnemann Medical School for two years.

"We stick closely to the SAT requirement of 1360, and also look for students with strong academics and medical or scientific research experience," she said. "We also want them to have an idea of what a doctor's life is like, not a romantic idea like on the television show ER."

Kugelman said it is hard to know which students to recommend, but her experience shows that medical schools have found a strong correlation between high SAT scores and students' later success in medical school. "You don't want to bring in students that won't do well," she said.

The attrition rate is very low, and most students in the program at Lehigh do go on to medical school. The numbers clearly show the competitiveness of the program.

Many students are drawn to Lehigh University and other colleges because of accelerated programs, Kugelman said, and each year 250 to 270 applicants apply. Seventy-five are offered interviews and 35 spots are offered. Usually around ten students accept.

Since so many students look virtually the same on paper, decisions are not easily made. The average student has SAT scores between 1400 to 1500, a challenging course load with as many Advanced Placement and honors class as possible, and experience like the National Youth Leadership Forum on Medicine, the Governor's School or shadowing doctors. Kugelman also looks for students who play sports, write for the school newspaper, sing in the musical, and were involved in extracurricular activities.

There is one requirement that is not easily ascertained from the application—the singular desire to become a doctor. Students must not have any doubts that this is what they want to do for the rest of their life. If a student has any doubts, Kugelman said the traditional way is best for them.

## Q&A

**What's the deal with the SAT cut-off?**
Traditional colleges let you know the average SAT scores of their students, and this is a good guide to see where you stand. Being below the mean is not a good sign, but then again, by definition, half the people accepted *are* below the average matriculant in terms of high school academics. While the SAT is a big factor, it isn't everything. Even Ivy League schools do not make distinctive SAT score requirements because they know that they will always make allowances for students who are exceptional in other areas, including but not limited to athletics.

On the flip side, combined programs let applicants know right from the start that they make *no* exceptions, and this is a good thing. It is important to have the most qualified applicants accepted because they are the ones who will be taking care of society's next generation.

Grades aren't the only important thing. The applicant pool for these programs are so strong that any program could easily fill its few spots with valedictorians boasting SAT scores above 1550, but they don't. It takes a lot more than geekish book smarts to make a good doctor, and they know that.

The main reason that there is an *application* SAT cut-off is that test taking skills are imperative to get through college and medical school. Accepting students who are unlikely to be successful in the program is self-defeating for the program goals, as well as the student.

For these reasons, the idea behind the cut-off is actually two-fold. It provides the schools with an easy filter to allow a more accurate assessment of the top-notch students. What it does for you, if you are below the given cut-off, is save you time that you would have wasted applying. Stating that students below a certain score don't have a chance may seem harsh, but it's honest. You can save yourself time and application fees by knowing that cut-off scores exist.

**What's more important: class rank or GPA?**
Programs usually have a minimum class rank requirement. So in that sense, if your academics are only par, meeting the necessary class rank is crucial to acceptance. Your GPA is not necessarily on the same scale as students from other schools. Colleges can give your grades their own score based on your transcript, but your class rank will usually suffice. However, this can be misleading, too, because you might be in a high school with exceptional students, making your rank relatively low compared to other applicants.

Standardized test scores will be necessary to represent everyone fairly by putting them on the same scale. These three values combined create an accurate academic profile.

**Does improvement count?**
Consistently strong scores all throughout high school is best, but if you've had a slow start, that doesn't necessarily mean that it's time to throw in the towel. If you have improved your grades throughout your high school career and can boast a strong junior and senior year, that will not be overlooked. You might even want to explain these struggles in your personal statement. Make sure that your overall rank meets the cut-off, though, because there will be no exception to this rule.

If, on the other hand, you start off strong and then fall during your senior year, this will not be ignored either. These programs are very competitive, and they have absolutely no reason to take a risk on someone who isn't willing to put in the work necessary to succeed, *especially* if they appear to be on a downward spiral.

### What about one low grade?

Despite how competitive these programs are, they still don't expect you to be perfect. Failure is something that everyone will face, whether they are prepared to handle it or not. Sometimes a transcript with character can have a positive effect. Concentrate on emphasizing your good qualities instead of worrying about a few low grades. Be prepared, though, to explain your mistakes. Questions like these are fair game during your interview.

### Isn't it difficult for admissions to decide what high school students will be like by the time they get to medical school?

Yes, it is very difficult to judge students based on their high school work. The best students are not always chosen, and many qualified students will be rejected. Many critics contend that students accepted to medical degree programs are not mature enough to handle medical school. However, students who are accepted to these programs are highly motivated and are distinguished from the typical college applicant in several ways. That is why they are selected.

Generally, the admission process selects students who will do well, but there are always some students who manage to slip through and really shouldn't be in the program. However, one must remember the highly competitive nature of accelerated programs. Initial selection is based on high school years, but final success is still contingent upon maintaining a certain GPA, passing the MCAT, etc. These checks along the way will help to filter out students who would not be successful in medical school before they get there.

### When applying, will I be competing with traditional applicants who are four years older?

No, you will not need a résumé as impressive as one from a college graduate because you will not be competing with them. Medical schools that offer combined programs will generally have a set number of seats set-aside for program students. These spots cannot be taken by traditional students no matter how strong their applicant pool may be compared to the feebleness of the high school students. Even when programmers don't fill spots set aside for them, the spots will be left vacant.

Although traditional students may not appreciate the fact that younger applicants are hurting their chances at acceptance, there is nothing they can do about it. If it bothers them that much, they can always apply to the majority of medical schools not affiliated with programs.

**So is it harder to make these programs or to make Ivy League schools?**
Both are extremely competitive. You may receive several acceptances from Ivy after Ivy, but not hear back from a single program, or vice versa.

# UNIT II

*Duty calls!*

# CHAPTER 4

## High School: Classes and Tests

*"Real knowledge is to know the extent of one's ignorance."*
—Confucius

*"As long as there are tests, there will be*
*prayer in public schools"*
—Bumper Sticker

You will apply for accelerated medical programs early during your senior year of high school. This does not mean that you need not think about it before this time. You will greatly increase your chances of being accepted by working on important aspects of your application all throughout high school. You will not be able to build a successful résumé in just a couple of months. Remember that everything you do will help in all your school applications, not just in medical program applications.

## Public School vs. Private School

Many students wonder whether the type of high school they attend affects their ability to gain entrance to an accelerated medical degree program. Generally speaking, it doesn't really matter where you go to high school, as long as you do well and have the qualities that accelerated medical program admissions officials are looking for.

Certain high schools *do* have a greater number of students that apply and that are accepted to medical degree programs. This trend can be attributed to counselors that make this option known to students, word of mouth, and medical programs that target specific school areas. For example, many accelerated programs are only to open to those students within a specific state. Other programs are open to anyone in the nation.

The majority of students who are accepted and matriculate into accelerated medical degree programs are from public high schools. However, that does not mean that if you attend a private high school, you will be at a disadvantage. Many students prefer private education for many reasons. A private school student, Christina, told us:

> *I think that the large, well-funded private schools give the same opportunities as public schools. I go to a small school though, and I feel like I miss out on some of the social aspects of high school (i.e. the prom, a big graduation, etc.). I think that my school has done a good job in preparing me to get into college, though.*

## Private High Schools:
- Private education instills values in a structured environment
- Students feel more comfortable learning in smaller class sizes
- Specific attention is more readily available
- There are resources not necessarily available to public schools
- More money may be available to some activities and sports

Here is another student's opinion:

> *I have found that private high schools better present the material and supply you with knowledge that will be needed in the medical profession. But public high schools give you a better perception of the real world and stations you might incur. Since I am attending high school and college at the same time I am involved in several programs at a variety of schools. Private schools are better if you already have a feel for the field, while public schools immerse you into many aspects at the same time.*
> *Jennifer L. Burns*

**Public High Schools:**
- Have students from various backgrounds (more real-world exposure)
- It's free
- There may be more programs and room for advancement
- More concentration is sometimes placed on the sciences and mathematics
- A wider variety of extra curricular activities may be available

## Course selection

Depending upon your high school, you may or may not have a lot of latitude in your course schedule. Generally, at least your first two years are predetermined, not including electives.

Many core courses including math, English, and the sciences are given with and without honors status. Since you are interested in accelerated medical programs, it is likely that you are an academic giant, and there is no reason that you wouldn't take all honors courses. Usually, these courses are weighted, which means they count more towards your GPA. A "B" in an honors course may count the same as an "A" in a regular level course.

Even if we are overestimating your academic prowess, it is always better to take the harder courses than playing it safe by taking easier ones. Getting straight A's in low-level courses doesn't prove anything about how you can handle a more rigorous schedule. This is exactly what you *do* need to prove to have a chance at getting accepted.

## AP courses

Advanced placement (AP) classes can really make a difference, not only in getting into a program, but in making your whole college experience easier. They don't make as much of a difference in the regular college application process.

Advanced placement classes will stand out on your high school transcript as classes that were taken by choice because you were qualified and advanced enough to fit them in to your schedule. They show that you made a conscious decision to challenge yourself and get a head start on your college career. It goes without saying that the AP sciences especially show your focus.

It is very important for admissions officials to accept people that they think can excel in the college science courses. These courses often act as weeding-out classes for traditional pre-meds. Doing well on these AP tests, which are written at a college level, can be the perfect way to show them that you are the candidate that they seek. The tests are scored on a scale from 1 to 5, with 5 being the highest.

You may only be able to take AP courses your senior year, but if you can take them earlier, do it. You should start planning early in high school to make schedules that will allow you to take many AP classes later on.

*I had AP biology during my junior year of high school and so my score of 5 was something that I could show the schools as a sign of my abilities.*

Jason Yanofski

### But what if my school doesn't offer any AP classes?

If your high school does not support advanced placement, this may negatively affect your application. Usually, not too much time is spent on any particular application, but if you are an overall strong candidate, your lack of AP courses may stand out as unusual. To get to the bottom of this mystery, admissions can look at your high school's profile and easily find out what AP classes they offer. If the school offered none or very few, then obviously there was nothing you could do, and they will see this.

Inability to take AP courses doesn't necessarily put you in a better position than an applicant who takes many AP classes and has a GPA that suffers because of it. While it's true that going to a school that is lacking in AP courses means that you can't take any, there is still no proof that you *would* have taken them, given the chance, and that you *would* have excelled.

### Other advantages of AP classes

Depending on which college you attend and which AP tests you take, you may be able to place out of certain college courses. You may get credit for scores of 3, 4, or 5. There are many reasons why using AP credit can make a difference once you get to college.

If you have required courses out of the way, this will give you a chance to take more non-science courses that interest you. You can opt for a minor or possibly a double major. You might also want to look into taking some time abroad or doing research. Another possibility is enrolling in more advanced science courses that will help get you the edge you'll want for medical school. Traditional students will have four years to take all the science courses they want, while you may only have two or three.

A different strategy at taking advantage of your extra credits would be just to lighten your load. This may be your chance to avoid spending your summer in the classroom, taking as few credits as possible one semester so that you can pledge a fraternity, or allow yourself more time on some of your difficult classes (physics or organic chemistry).

If you are in an accelerated program, it is likely that you have an accelerated mindset. Be wary, though, about advancing too fast. You can't start medical school as soon as you finish your college requirements, and if you are done midyear you will not necessarily be given the second semester off. You'll be forced to remain a full time student and will just be taking unnecessary classes.

Taking AP courses in high school definitely enhances your application, and having 4's or 5's on AP tests shows important strengths, too. Also, there are national awards given out based on good scores on a certain numbers of AP tests.

## Grades

High school is not hard for everyone, but it *will* take dedication to get consistent good grades. For study tips, etc., see Chapter 14.

## Standardized tests

Academics around the US are not always comparable. Some high schools emphasize more science than math. Others emphasize linguistics and speech more than music, etc. Thus, in order to have a fair system of gauging students' skills, standardized tests come into play.

Though we all loathe sharpening #2 pencils and Saturday mornings spent taking those pressure-packed exams, it is a reality that we must all face at some point. In the next chapter, we will highlight extra-curricular activities that enable you to demonstrate your talents, skills, and passion. You should view standardized tests in the same light. You will be able to present a better picture of yourself to admissions officials with every standardized test you take. Let's take a look at a few of these tests.

## SAT

The Scholastic Aptitude Test is a very important test, which can be looked at in two different ways. Your goal may be to get a super high score, or it might be just to get the scores necessary to apply. A score of 1400 may be low relative to other applicants, but it is not perceived as low by admissions. In fact, there is a point in the admissions process where scores are not looked at any more and where everyone is put on an equal playing field.

**What is the format of the test?**
There are two types of sections: verbal and math. The maximum score for each section is 800, and both scores are added together to make a total possible score of 1600. The test is given several times

a year on Saturday mornings, and it takes about three hours to complete.

All of the verbal questions and most of the math questions are multiple choice. Calculators are permitted, though only on the math sections. For most questions, calculators may actually slow you down.

## Verbal

The three types of verbal questions are analogies, sentence completions, and critical reading questions. Analogies and sentence completions both require an extensive vocabulary to do well on, as well as a logical mind. Critical reading questions test your reading and comprehension abilities. In this section, it is still possible to get a perfect score if only a few questions are missed.

## Math

The three types of math questions are multiple choice, grid-ins, and quantitative comparisons. Grid-ins are questions in which you must solve and write in your own answer, and quantitative comparisons involve determining a relationship between expressions in two different columns. You will have to choose whether column A is greater than or less than column B, whether they are equal, or whether a relationship cannot be determined from the information provided. You will need to get every question correct in this section to score 800.

## Preparation

The way to go about studying for the SAT is first to become aware of exactly what you need to know. The math *concepts* are not too difficult, though the questions may be very tricky because of the way in which they are presented. For the verbal portion of the test, if you don't have a good vocabulary, it's time to get one. Reading classics will allow you to encounter many SAT words, and so will reading the newspaper regularly.

Reading books, magazines (*Time, U.S. News, Newsweek, Popu-*

*lar Science, Scientific American,* etc.), and newspapers (*The New York Times, The Wall Street Journal,* etc.) with a dictionary at hand is a good long-term approach, but if the test is in a few months (or tomorrow!!!), your best bet is to learn directly from a list of about 200 words. Once you've learned the material, take as many practice tests as you can, and always look at why you got questions wrong.

There are many commercial courses available to you (The Princeton Review, etc.). If you don't mind paying the money, these courses can be a good source of motivation. They will provide you with practice tests and simulated testing conditions. Unfortunately, most of the guidance usually only involves test-taking tactics (guessing strategy). This kind of advice can be found in books available for a small fraction of the price. Hey, wait a second, this is a book!

### Guessing and strategy

You do get more points for a question if it's left blank than if it is answered wrong. However, statistically you *should* guess if you can eliminate at least one answer choice, and if you can eliminate more than one, it is definitely in your best interest to guess. Most likely, you will be able to eliminate answers for logical reasons even if you don't know how to fully answer the question.

During the test, the worst thing that you can do is to skip a bubble and find out that due to one error, every answer is in the wrong spot. To avoid this problem, you may want to transfer blocks of about five answers from the test sheet to the answer sheet so this forces you to periodically check your position.

Don't spend too much time on any particular question. Just keep moving through the test. If you have time at the end of a section, go back and check over your work. If you find any mistakes, you'll be glad you did. However, if you can't decide between two answers, your first instinct will usually be correct.

### Test day

You should have been preparing and practicing for the SAT for a long time. Don't worry about it on the night before the test. Get together everything that you will need so that you don't have any trouble finding anything the next morning. These things include any necessary paperwork, your ID, a few #2 pencils, your calculator, suitable clothing, and a light snack.

Get a good night's rest. If you can't fall asleep, don't look at the clock, and don't take any medication. You'll fall asleep eventually. When you are finished with the test, take a break from everything for a few days if you can. You deserve it!

## Other Standardized Tests

Almost all programs require an SAT score, while other tests are usually not required. However, if you didn't do as well as you wanted to on the SAT, you might consider taking more tests to balance out your score and help your application.

### ACT

The ACT Assessment (administered by American College Testing) measures skills in four areas: English, mathematics, reading, and science reasoning. It lasts two hours and 55 minutes.

For those of you that are more science oriented and want to take a test that requires some background knowledge, the ACT may be for you. Many high caliber students prefer the ACT to the SAT because they view the SAT as a test where no studying is necessary. Alternatively, the ACT tests for a strong background in the sciences.

### SAT II

This test was formerly called the Achievement Test. The educational testing service (ETS) conducts the SAT II. They are the same people that bring you the SAT I (bet you didn't see that coming!). The SAT II subject test is an hour exam measuring specific knowledge in a particular area.

The following 17 subjects are offered: Writing, Literature,

American History and Social Studies, World History, Level I Math, Level IIC Math, French, German, Modern Hebrew, Italian, Latin, Spanish, Chinese, Japanese, Biology, Chemistry, Physics. You may take up to three subject tests in one sitting.

SAT II tests are highly specific in particular subject areas. It is good to take an SAT II in at least one of the three major fields: English, science, and mathematics. Take them in the subjects you are strongest in. It is also highly recommended that you take the SAT II right after you have the course in high school so that it is fresh in your mind. For example, if you are taking AP History, take the SAT II test in history right after the AP exam. Contact your specific medical program of interest to find out which tests they recommend.

## Courses at local colleges

Many students take advantage of getting a little bit of college under their belt early on. Many of the advantages of this parallel those of taking AP courses. Not only does it show maturity and dedication, but it can also be very practical. Here's what one high school student had to say on the matter:

> I'm currently a high school senior doubly enrolled at Chaminade High School and Long Island University. Through a special program in my high school, I will earn 37 college credits by the time I graduate. I'm doing this partially because I'm interested in going to medical school, and I understand that the road for medical training is lengthy, indeed.
>
> Christopher Adams

# CHAPTER 5

## High School: Extra Curriculars and Summer Programs

*"Keep away from people who try to belittle your ambitions. Small people always do that, but the really great make you feel that you, too, can become great."*
—Mark Twain

*"I don't want to join the kind of a club that accepts people like me as members."*
—Groucho Marx

As long as you don't lose your focus, high school can be relatively easy. In general, the gifted student will find that he can get A's with only a minimal amount of studying and still have a lot of free time. Getting good grades and test scores is important, but it's going to take a lot more than that to get into an accelerated medical program.

You will need to be active. As far as extra curricular activities are concerned, you can't just go through the motions. There are plenty of student council presidents and school paper editors, but very few spots in the combined program of your choice. You need to show some initiative and do something that will represent your best qualities.

Though there is no way to guarantee acceptance into an accelerated medical program, this chapter will focus on what you must do and be involved with in order to stand a good chance. It will give you a better picture of the kinds of activities that programmers have engaged in to get where they are today.

Many people are under the misconception that a 4.0 GPA and 1600 SAT score alone will guarantee acceptance into an accelerated medical programs, but this couldn't be farther from the truth. These programs are seeking to obtain a wide variety of diverse and well-rounded individuals to be doctors.

Although GPA and SAT scores are important, they will never be the clinching factors. They draw attention to an application, but extra curricular activities are what take over from there. You must work hard outside the classroom as well as within. In this chapter, we will examine several routes of doing so.

## The formula

The basic formula includes at least one of each of the following: research experience, leadership role, job experience, meaningful volunteering, and experience within the medical field. These experiences can be combined. For example, riding as an EMT (emergency medical technician) would immediately show meaningful volunteering and experience within the medical field. However, working behind the desk at a hospital doesn't necessarily show either of these traits.

## Types of activities

You should be thinking about what characteristics you would be able to prove by the activities that you participate in. For example, take the initiative to start a new club in your school. It doesn't matter how many people join or show up to meetings. *Details aren't put on your transcript, and they aren't always important.* What will be seen is that you founded a club by yourself, and you will come off as the ambitious and motivated individual that you are.

## Scholastic activities

Scholastic activities demonstrate your knowledge outside the classroom. It is one thing to get A's on all your English essays, but it's another thing to win debates because you can formulate logical, eloquent arguments impromptu. Medical schools can easily narrow the field by weeding out the "bookworms" from the "leaders of tomorrow." These activities bring attention to you and say, "Look at me, I can apply what I learned in a foreign setting."

This is the kind of skill that is called upon doctors on a daily basis. Tests measure your intelligence on paper, but these activities bring that intelligence to life. Also, winning some academic competitions, awards, and tournaments certainly wouldn't hurt your résumé.

- Debate, speech team (forensics)
- Student senate
- Math team
- Science olympiad
- School paper
- Language club (Spanish, French, etc.)
- Honor society
- Chess team
- Publishing essays, etc.
- Research

Here, a college sophomore recounts his high school research experience:

> *During my freshman year in high school I applied to a unique program called the "Westinghouse Research Program." It entailed several years of preparation, culminating in the development of an independent research project. The program started second semester freshman year with a research methods class and a special biology class.*
>
> *Sophomore year was similar with two more research method*

*classes each semester and a special chemistry class. Then, during junior year we began our search for a lab to work in. Living in New York City offered almost endless possibilities.*

*Once we found a lab, the director or one of the researchers in the lab would become our mentor. We would work at the lab anywhere from 6-18 months, depending on how early we found it. When the time came, we began writing our papers. The result of all our work was a 20-page paper documenting our individual research. We then submitted our papers to the national competition.*

*There is a rivalry among several New York City high schools around this competition, my school being one of the several. In the recent years, including the year I entered, my school has fared quite well. I value the experience as very beneficial. As well, the 20-page paper was a nice supplement to my college applications, and I included it with all my applications, demonstrating my research skills and talents. Anyone from anywhere in the country can submit an entry. Just keep in the mind the name of the competition has been changed to "Intel Science Talent Search."*

Oren Marciano

Here is a description of a research program that high school senior, Quinn, is currently involved in:

*I'm a senior in high school in East Los Angeles. I belong to a spectacular program that chooses about 22 students from about one hundred applicants. The USC Science, Technology and Research (STAR) program allows these students to work in a lab affiliated with the USC Health Science Campus. We get the chance to work with a research team while conducting our own scientific project. I can definitely say that it is a great experience. It is a big commitment, but I've managed to keep focused and on the right track.*

*It has always been a dream of mine to go into medicine. I figured that if I joined the STAR program, the experience of working in a lab would help me decide if I liked working behind the fume hood glass for the rest of my life. I still want to go into medicine, and I plan to do so once I graduate from high school, but I wouldn't mind being in someone's lab in between.*

## Medical related activities

So, you want to be a doctor? PROVE IT! That is what medical schools will be looking for, and you will need to show them your dedication. Many students are not even considered for accelerated programs because they lack "medical exposure" in high school. Your interest in medicine must be genuine. In addition, these activities will help you figure out if you really want to be a doctor. After all, you are being asked to make a decision that many individuals make during their later college years.

You must find out all you can about the medical profession before accepting a position in a program. If while working at a hospital, you learn that you puke at the sight of blood or start to break into convulsions from the smell of latex, it may be a sign that medicine isn't your bag, baby!

· EMT riding
· Volunteering at a hospital
· Medical internship
· Shadowing a doctor
· Attending science symposiums and lectures
· Keeping up with medical news – (reading *JAMA, Cell, Nature, New England Journal of Medicine,* etc.)

A college freshman shares his experience with us:

*I went to a pre-med forum at Berkeley last summer, the National Youth Leadership Forum on Medicine. I loved the program. It was great to meet so many motivated students who were interested in medicine. We attended numerous presentations by respected physicians from various fields. The forum was divided into groups of around 20 with a medical student advisor. It was really great to be able to talk with someone who was in med. school.*

*Our group met with numerous doctors and even an HIV patient. It was interesting to actually speak with someone who had the virus, and get his perspective on the medical field and life itself.*

*We also visited UC Davis medical school and were allowed to participate in numerous different labs, including the morgue, which was extremely interesting. I'm sure it looks pretty good on my résumé and shows people, and medical schools specifically, my motivation. However, what I gained personally in experience was far more important than how it looks on my résumé.*

*It really helped give the abstract idea of being a doctor a more concrete feeling. Many people there also decided that medicine was not their field from their experiences at the forum.*

## Sports

Before you start a vigorous training regimen, let us remind you that sports can be helpful even if it doesn't appear that you are going to become the next Michael Jordan any time soon. Sports illustrate that you are well-rounded. This sets up your appearance as the "renaissance" individual that admissions officials are looking for. If you can run like the wind, score 50+ points in a basketball game, etc., we encourage you to develop that talent and make sure it is clearly noted on your application.

However, if you're like most people, simply partaking in a sport (even on a recreational basis) is good enough for all intensive purposes. The message that you want to get across is that you are more than just a brain. You are dynamic, extroverted, and willing to challenge yourself physically as well as mentally.

Admissions officials will prefer applicants who can play a sport *and* balance the books. There is also a lot of opportunity to show leadership when on a team, especially if you can make the position of captain by your junior or senior year. Sports define your ability to work with others, deal with victory and defeat, and build character and sportsmanship. Such experience is invaluable in your life as well as your medical career because not every attempt at life saving will end up victorious.

- Track, tennis, high school sports
- Varsity, intramural, or recreational
- Team or individual based
- Assisting at sporting events
- Organizing a club sport

### Instruments/Fine arts

Not all of us are musically inclined. However, learning the basics of piano or attending a few classical concerts can be quite enriching. These activities reveal your artistic and cosmopolitan appeal to prospective medical schools. Learning an instrument when you have time in high school is much easier than at a later stage in life when you are bombarded with many responsibilities. Many of us find that such musical diversions are a way to relieve stress and deal with the problems of everyday life – filling out college applications!

- Piano, drums, guitar, etc.
- Chorus
- Recitals and public performances
- Dance (ballet, etc.)
- Painting
- Attending shows/musicals
- Museum internships

### Service

It will probably be difficult to get very far in the medical application process without some form of volunteerism, and will be worthwhile. As a doctor, it will be your duty to do help others, and learning to do so early on will develop social skills and acquaint you with the "service" aspect of the medical profession.

Unlike sports and instruments, a lack of service might be held against you in the selection process. Service can be obtained on various levels. It can be something as simple as publicizing a fundraiser or more challenging as organizing one yourself. The degree of service depends on how much time and effort you have available.

- Volunteer (Red Cross, Salvation Army, local hospital, etc.)
- Soup kitchens
- Food drives
- Clothing drives
- Fundraisers
- Helping relief causes

Volunteering can be extremely meaningful as well. Here's what a Colorado high school sophomore told us when asked why she volunteers:

> *I love volunteering at my hospital. I specifically asked to volunteer in obstetrics because I love babies, and I think it is such a miracle how they come into the world. I provide my time because it will greatly help my future. Since I am only 15, it is hard for me to get a job because employers only hire 16 and above, so when I turn 16, I will have some work on my record, which will make me more appealing to admissions.*
>
> *My high school offers credit for 72.5 hours (the length of one semester) of community service. In the long run, volunteer work looks really good on college applications; it shows a dedication to the community. The other reason I volunteer is because I want to give back to my community. I believe that everyone takes a lot from their environment and we should all give back at least some of what we've taken. Since I haven't had any formal medical training, I am usually only able to do filing, stocking,*

*and answering the phones, but once in a while I get a chance to work with the babies.*

*Every time I see a baby, I always think of a little story I heard when I was young. Before a child is born, an angel puts their finger up to their mouth and says, "Sh, don't tell." That explains the little crease under our nose. This is why I volunteer.*

## Leadership

Leadership is a quality that grows when nurtured. The seed must be planted through activities that place you in a position of respect and responsibility. As a leader, you are forced to consider the consequences of actions based on several factors. It is this "take charge" attitude that defines doctors in their profession.

Doctors pave the path for medicine in society and its benefits. Being timid and lacking initiative will not bode well for future doctors. In emergency situations, when people's lives are on the line, you must be willing to be assertive and commanding. We all have that capacity. Make sure you realize yours.

Look for ethnic clubs and other activities where you may be able to eventually earn a position on council. Also look to national service clubs, such as the Rotary, Kiwanis, and Lions organizations. These groups are often affiliated with high school chapter clubs. They'll help you get started and may even provide funding. If your school is not currently participating, this is a good opportunity for you to get involved with something important. Because professionals from your community run these clubs, you may be able to make some great connections as well.

- Captain of anything (sports/academic)
- School president, student body positions
- Founder of anything

## Job experience

Working after school or during summers shows maturity and commitment. You may work because you need to financially, or you may want to build up your savings. Either way, if you work long enough to be promoted, you may find yourself in a position of leadership and responsibility, two key qualities that you want to express.

You can also combine different parts of the formula by getting a job within the medical field. You could do this by working with a doctor or nurse as an assistant or doing paper work. You may also be able work in environments such as nursing homes, homeless shelters, or rehabilitation centers. Research centers sometimes offer pay positions for assistants on large projects.

Jobs with professionals can be great ways to get meaningful recommendations. Your application will be strengthened if an MD says that he supports and recommends you because of the qualities that he's seen you possess while working with him. Don't underestimate simpler jobs, however, especially ones that allow you to work with children.

- In an office
- Assistant to a professional
- Hospital
- Research center
- Tutor
- Babysitting
- Start your own business

## Q&A

**Will I go farther with quality or quantity?**
Rather than being concerned with the number of activities, you should focus on quality. Being involved with 4-5 solid activities will definitely distinguish you from someone with 25 activities listed, including everything from basket weaving to professional lawn mowing. In addition, being focused allows you to do well and exceed in these activities.

You should select activities that pique your interest in areas that you enjoy and thereby can better demonstrate your talents, skills, and personality. College student Paul Kursky of Brandeis University agrees: "Usually, if you join a club because you are genuinely interested and become progressively more involved in that club over time, application review committees will appreciate the effort you've made."

### Should I engage in activities just to help my application?

The answer to this is no, but only because it his hard to succeed when there is no motivation. There is no single activity that is necessary in order to gain acceptance to a program, so you have the leverage to choose what interests you most.

Building up your résumé is something of which you should always be conscious. If it's not as impressive as you'd like it to be, then you are not as active as you should be. Chapter Seven and Chapter Eight will talk about how to express to admissions everything you've done—via your résumé, essays, and recommendations.

## Summer programs

While your friends are relaxing and enjoying the summer, it will be difficult for you to even think about schoolwork, but participating in a summer program will show admissions that you are dedicated and focused within the fields of science. Rudyard Kaplan, a college sophomore, was kind enough to enlighten us with an evaluation of the summer program that he attended and what it meant to him:

> *One way to determine if the rigors of practicing medicine are right for you is to attend one of the growing number of pre-college summer programs geared toward future doctors. I attended one such program at Brown University entitled "So You Think You Want to be a Doctor?" and found it to be one of the most influential summers of my high school career. The Brown pro-*

gram is a complete "mini-medical school" that combines many aspects of real medical school into a rigorous five-week program. Participants experience everything from cadaver dissections to anatomy lectures to doctor tagalongs, all pre-arranged by the course instructor.

I, along with most of my fellow "campers," felt the Brown program helped to cement my desire to become a doctor. Many participants, however, felt that just the opposite was true, saying that the program helped them to come to the early realization that they should consider alternate career options. One friend of mine who attended the program with me became so ill during the cadaver dissection that he decided to study political science instead of biology in college.

Summer programs have numerous benefits in addition to helping students decide if medicine is the right career choice. Not only does a summer program look good on a college application résumé, but it also provides the invaluable experience of dorm living. One of the hardest adjustments you will make at college is living with a roommate for the first time. Experiencing dorm living prior to arriving at college will help you get used to living in such a small room with a complete stranger. The advantage of having your first roommate experience during the summer is that you have nothing to lose if the relationship turns sour. Once you are at college, however, you will have your grades to worry about.

Another seldom-mentioned benefit of attending a summer program is the connections you will make with practicing doctors. When you are assigned to a doctor as a tagalong, you will spend several days observing every part of that doctor's routine, from hospital rotations to office checkups. At the end of the tagalong it is very easy to remain in touch with the doctor throughout the college application process. The advice that the doctor I shadowed has given me has been priceless, and I have remained in touch with him to this day.

*Summer programs are not cheap, often costing upwards of*
*$5,000. Keep in mind, however, that many offer scholarships*
*as well as low-interest educational loans.*

*Whether you are trying to determine if medicine is right for*
*you, or you just want to get a feel for what college will be like, a*
*summer program may be a wise investment in your future.*
*Admission into the programs is often competitive, but can vary*
*depending on their individual reputations. Further informa-*
*tion and application forms can be found on the web or through*
*your guidance counselor.*

Through summer programs, you are taught a variety of laboratory techniques and communication and problem solving skills,
exposing you to college life at a young age. In Appendix C, you
will find a list of summer programs and a piece by David Reibstein,
founder of the Penn Summer Science Academy.

Another route is to independently secure internships and research positions during the summer. Many students do this during the summer before senior year. They may have spent previous
summers in programs at universities to learn the proper skills, and
now they are ready to work on their own. Obtaining a research
position is sometimes more difficult than being accepted into a
summer program. Here are some tips to help you secure one:

· Make a list of local research institutions. These include
  hospitals, universities, and research centers. Use the Internet
  to assist you.
· Find out names of research directors and individuals working
  at these institutions. Using a database or your local library,
  find out what papers they have published. Get your hands
  on these papers and read them thoroughly. This alone will
  help you learn important research skills! They may seem
  complicated, so ask an older friend with science knowledge
  or a college student to help you.

- Arrange a meeting with these research individuals. You may be able to contact them through e-mail, phone, or just by walking into their office. Be sure to mention that you have read their work and are interested in joining them in their research. You must show a genuine interest in what they are doing.
- Before you meet with researchers, have a transcript and résumé ready to show them. Make sure it is pristine and exemplifies your skills in the scientific field.
- Do not be discouraged if you are turned down at first. Keep trying until you find someone who is willing to take you, even if this requires several phone calls and meetings. Your hard work is sure to pay off.
- Start the whole process in February or March. Waiting until the last minute will mean that other students are likely to have already taken up available positions, and remember that researchers have *no obligation* to give you a position.
- Make sure you have proper working forms and permits if you are not of working age. This may take weeks to obtain.

There are several benefits that come from summer research internships. The obvious one is that you learn lab skills and are exposed to research first hand. You may also be able to publish a paper in a reputed medical journal along with your medical research director if you have contributed significantly to the project.

If you plan to compete in science competitions such as Intel, you may be able to design an experiment while in your research position. After working in the lab, the research director will be a great source for letters of recommendation.

So now that you understand the importance of extra curricular activities, get your head out of this book and go do something productive. Your résumé is looking pretty thin! But make sure you come back eventually to finish reading the rest. You won't stand a chance at surviving your interview without our help. Oh yeah, and we haven't even taught you how to *write* your résumé yet!

# UNIT III

## Why? Why? . . . Why?!

# CHAPTER 6

## The Application Process and Timeline

*"Any change, even a change for the better, is always accompanied by drawbacks and discomforts."*
—Arnold Bennett

*"Every man has his own destiny: the only imperative is to follow it, to accept it, no matter where it leads him."*
—Henry Miller

You've decided that accelerated medical programs are for you, and you've worked hard all throughout high school. Now it's your senior year and it's finally time to apply. See Appendix A for specific instructions on how to contact the schools directly.

## Steps of the application

To apply to programs, you need to get the standard application from the participating undergraduate university. There should be information about the program and what sections you need to fill out in order to qualify. Many programs will ask for additional essays.

You have to remember that assuming you make your way through the process, the same application gets passed along. That means that you may find yourself on an interview where the essay that you wrote early on unexpectedly resurfaces. Remember what you wrote and keep copies for later review.

The application is initially sent to the undergraduate college. They then forward it to the medical school, and the final step is the interview there.

When the medical school is affiliated with the undergraduate department of a different university, the college initially reviews applications. The college may or may not want to interview you, and sometimes they use this to filter out less qualified students. Generally, candidates who meet the program requirements get their applications sent to the medical school.

The college interview should be informative. Ask them any questions you have about the particular program you are applying to. They may be able to give you advice and tell you where they think you stand. They have a definite interest in your acceptance to the program.

Once the application is forwarded on, the university really doesn't have any say in who is accepted and who isn't. Anything they tell you about what the medical school is looking for should be taken seriously. Remember that they have been involved in the process for years, and they will have an idea what kinds of students have the best chance at making it to the interview and beyond.

You will get a call or receive a letter if you have made it to the interview stage. This is a big hurdle, and a large percentage of the original pool of applicants has been weeded out by this point. If your interview is successful, the next thing you'll get in the mail is news from the school that you've been accepted, rejected, or put onto the waiting list.

## Picking programs

You should apply to as many programs as you can afford, but don't waste your time applying to ones that you wouldn't want to go to. Many of the applications are similar, but don't be tempted to toss aside applications that ask for a unique essay. There are no guarantees of acceptance anywhere and sending out multiple applications increases your odds at getting accepted to at least one program. If you gain acceptance to multiple programs, then you can look at where you really want to be, and who is offering you the best package, financial and otherwise.

> *I applied to multiple BA/MD programs, and it was very time consuming. I had to first apply for regular admission and then to the BA/MD program. But I still think that it is worth it because if I do get accepted into the program, then I won't have to worry about applying for medical school later on.*
>
> *The biggest problem that I faced was the lack of information about the schools that have these programs. It would also help if the colleges provided information about the average student who gets accepted into the program. I had to call each school individually to find out my chances of getting accepted.*
>
> *Megha Patel*

Sounds like Megha could have used our book! Use the factors explained in Chapter One to determine what is most important to you. Then, see our profiles section and order brochures from all the schools that you are interested in. This detective work will allow you to become an informed applicant.

## Applying only to programs

Nobody should apply only to programs, because they could get burned. Always apply to other schools as well, no matter how impressive you are as a candidate.

## Location

If you know that you need to stay close to home, then there is no reason to apply to schools out of state. However, if you are really dedicated, you may be willing to fly across the country. You may also have a preference as far as the environment surrounding the school, which will affect your lifestyle. Here, Tom Cortese, a sophomore at George Washington University makes a comparison between going to school in a small town and going to school in the city:

> *Generally, a suburban campus brings with it the comfort of a contained, self-sufficient environment with little to no interference from outside elements. Such campuses tend to be somewhat safer environments and may also encourage more peer interactions among students outside of the classroom. However, this type of environment makes it difficult to extend yourself beyond the campus. Therefore, one may feel trapped.*
>
> *Of the advantages that arise from a city campus, probably the most important is the ability to utilize the resources within the city along with the resources within the school. Attending a city school allows you the ability to explore concepts in a non-school setting. Health clinics, hospitals, and doctor's offices, as well as a host of other professional establishments are typically welcoming of student internships. Furthermore, such resources may be helpful, simply for finding the answers to your questions.*
>
> *Cities also may provide for unwanted hassle or confusion. Many city campuses are spread out in all directions, forcing students to use buses or other means of transportation to get around. You may also find yourself overwhelmed by the grandeur of the city, and feel more at ease in a contained environment.*
>
> *Both the city and the suburb provide for their own characteristic benefits and downfalls. Choosing between the two is simply contingent on where you feel most comfortable.*

## Timeline

In preparation for application to accelerated and combined degree medical programs, timing holds vital significance. Engaging in the right actions at the proper time will ensure success. Many students find themselves at a disadvantage when it comes time to apply to accelerated and combined degree programs simply because they didn't take that extra AP course or SAT II during their previous year. Some may have overlooked that summer internship or research experience.

Many students mourn the time they wasted during their freshmen and sophomore years of high school, goofing off. Lucky for you, our book will put you on the right track!

In college, you will have *less* time to do *more* work. High school will seem like a "breeze" to most students when compared with college life. However, the foundations of your ability to do college level work has its roots in high school. High school must be viewed as a transition period towards higher education. Good study skills and test taking mentality do not come overnight; they must be developed over years of hard work and practice.

## Freshmen and Sophomore Year

While your friends are relaxing during these early years, it is your opportunity to get ahead of the game. The best service you can do for yourself is to start preparing for college early.

Many students think that it is too early to worry about college during their freshmen year in high school. They are wrong; you can never start too early. Once you get ahead, it will be difficult for others to catch up. These are also the years when you have a great deal of free time, and you should use it wisely.

Your courses during these two years, compared with the upcoming years, are relatively less difficult. Try your best to get good grades because this will help your overall GPA. Ironically, these are the years that sometimes separate the valedictorians from the salutatorians. To avoid working every day of your junior and senior year and worrying whether or not you are in the top five percent of your class, work hard now to assure yourself that you will be. Here are some things to keep in mind during these critical years:

- Take a strong courseload rich in science, math, and English. A good doctor will require the knowledge gained from these subjects throughout his career. These are also areas highly tested on standardized exams. Remedying problem spots now will guarantee success later on.

- Save certain electives that might hurt your GPA for senior year. A high GPA is vital for admission to an accelerated medical program. If you know that a certain music or art teacher is notorious for giving out B's and C's, avoid him or her at all costs. Every point makes a difference.
- Learn how to study, and identify weaknesses in your study habits in order to strengthen them. Becoming an effective studier will ensure success throughout the rest of your life. (See Chapter 14)
- Read beyond assigned coursework. This will add depth to your knowledge.
- Read novels and newspaper editorials. Not only will reading help your comprehension skills, but it will make you a more sophisticated person, increase your vocabulary, and set you apart from others during college interviews.
- Build your vocabulary by reading and studying SAT words. Work them into your everyday language.
- Write poetry, essays, and book reviews, and send them into competitions. Doing this early on will make sure you have an amazing résumé when application time rolls around.
- Sign up for community groups and clubs, such as student government, band, etc. This will allow you to attain leadership positions (president or captain) by the time you apply for programs.
- Volunteer at a hospital and read more about the medical profession. These are the vital years during which you will discover whether or not you truly want to become a doctor.
- Meet with your counselor. Bring our book along in case she isn't aware of accelerated and combined degree programs, as many counselors are unaware of these options.
- Get an organizer and date book to keep track of your appointments and deadlines.
- Talk with older students about future classes. Learn from their mistakes and successes.

- Consider getting a job that will not interfere with school-work.
- Talk to family members about college and medical programs. Starting discussions early will help avoid the disputes that may arise as to where you should go to college.
- Read about summer programs. (See Appendix C)
- Plan what AP courses you are going to take during your junior and senior year. If your school does not offer AP courses, many local community colleges and universities offer them. Find out how you can register and receive credit for both high school and college. Medical programs look very favorably upon AP and college level classes. (See Chapter 4)

**Junior Year**

Junior year is very intense. This is the year that will make or break you when it becomes time to apply to colleges, because these grades receive the most scrutiny. Since you are taking Advanced Placement classes and a more difficult courseload, it may be harder to get A's. This is also the year when the PSAT and the SAT must be taken.

You can't afford to take this year lightly because a lot is riding on it. Now is the time when you must decide whether or not you are going to apply to accelerated medical programs. (See Chapters 1,2) Remember that the choice to become a doctor is not made by most people until late during their college career, and you are considering it four to five years earlier. Here are things to follow to make junior life a little easier:

September
- Register for the PSAT. Waivers are available for those who face financial hardships. Ask your counselor for more information. This test is important for two reasons: It is a good predictor of performance on the SAT, and many scholarships (National Merit Scholarship Awards, etc.) are awarded on the basis of PSAT scores.

- Begin your college search and find out more about accelerated and combined degree medical programs. Use our book as guidance.
- Attend college fairs; these are where college and university representatives come to high schools and advertise their respective schools.
- Continue your activities and gain leadership positions.
- Arrange a meeting with your counselor to go over your transcript. Make sure the proper number of credits has been earned for graduation. Are you missing any classes?
- Learn the application jargon and acronyms.

October
- PSAT TIME! Get those #2 pencils ready.
- Contact medical schools to find out specific requirements for programs that interest you. Every year there may be slight changes.

November-December
- Look into other traditional colleges.
- Get demographics and statistics on schools.
- Consider a safety school.

January-February
- Start to prepare for the SAT, SAT II's, ACT, etc.
- Consider an SAT prep course such as Kaplan or the Princeton Review. Medical programs are extremely competitive and higher scores put you in a better position to get in.

March-April
- Register for the SAT and ACT.
- Make a list of colleges (medical programs and traditional) that you wish to apply to.

- Plan college campus visits on your own and through your high school.
- Register for SAT II subject tests. These are required for almost all medical programs. It is crucial that you do well on these difficult tests.
- Sign up for a summer program.

May-August
- Take your AP tests.
- Take the SAT, ACT, and SAT II tests.
- Contact colleges to get on mailing lists to receive applications. Request videos and multimedia handouts by the university.
- Apply for scholarships and grants.
- Begin writing the dreaded college essays. (See Chapter 7)
- Consider and contact teachers for letters of reference.

**Senior Year**
Senior year is filled with anxiety over where you'll be after graduation. Organization is key. You might send out several applications and need a dozen or more letters of recommendation. Make sure you keep copies of important documents and a timetable of deadlines. Get Mom or Pop to help you get organized if you feel that you can't handle it on your own. Late or sloppy applications will almost always be overlooked. Here is how you can avoid that:

September
- Make a résumé listing your activities, awards, etc. (See Chapter 7)
- Hand out requests for letters of recommendation.
- Start college applications.
- If you plan to take the SAT, ACT, SAT II again, register now.
- Narrow down the number of schools and medical programs to which you are going to apply.

- Make a timeline listing application and financial aid deadlines.
- Be sure to keep copies of applications and important documents.
- Remember that applications to medical programs are due earlier than those of traditional colleges.

October-December
- Retake the SAT or ACT if you feel your scores are not adequate for admission to your desired college or program. Do not take the test again if you don't feel your scores will improve because colleges see all of your scores. SAT II tests have score choice, and this allows you to see your scores and release only the ones of your choice.
- Send out completed applications through your high school. Fee waivers may be available. Keep copies of sent items.
- Set up college interviews with alumni in your area or contact the university directly. (See Chapter 9)
- Look up further financial aid information.

January
- Complete FAFSA and state aid forms. Keep copies!
- Make sure your high school sends out mid-year reports to your colleges.
- Wait anxiously for replies from programs and colleges.

April-June
- Take AP tests.
- Receive acceptances, rejections, and wait lists.
- Decide where you want to go, and respond before the deadline.
- Send deposits to the college for housing and tuition.

July-August
· Relax and enjoy your last summer before college.
· Make sure you are ready to start school in the fall. (See Chapter 11)

# CHAPTER 7

## Essays, the Personal Statement, and the Résumé

*"The reason that there are so few good books written is that so
few people who write know anything."*
—Walter Bagehot

*"I stand by all the misstatements that I've made."*
—Dan Quayle

College application essays strike fear into the hearts of all college
applicants. Other parts of the application are relatively simple to
fill out because of their objectivity. When it comes to fields for
your name and address, you know what the answers are – hopefully! Unfortunately, when it comes to essays, even the best writers
can face an impenetrable mental block.

Unlike those essays written overnight for AP English, these
aren't graded. In fact, they are viewed in an entirely different perspective. Besides being well organized, grammatically correct,
proofread, and coherent, a college essay must provide the reader
with insight to your personality. It's your chance to distinguish yourself from other applicants. It goes without saying
that waiting until the last minute to start writing would be to
your disadvantage.

Many applications come with multiple questions, and they

may allow you some choice. Here are some sample questions you may encounter:

- What is a significant experience in your life?
- Who influenced your life the most?
- Why do you want to become a doctor?
- If you could meet anyone, who would it be and why?
- Make your own question and answer it.

Remember that the point of the essay is to reveal who you are to the admissions committee. View these questions as a vehicle to express yourself. Don't waste time explaining what a doctor does in society or what your role-model wears on a daily basis. Admissions officials either already know that information or don't really care. It would be more suitable to write about what you have learned from your mentor and how you applied it in another situation.

You won't get anywhere if your responses are not interesting. Admissions officials have read a million essays about students who want to become a doctor either because they want to help people, because they like biology, or because they just didn't know what else to do. Rick Bleakley told us this:

> I wrote my college essay on why I wanted to be a physician using a caption I had written for a drawing I drew in elementary school. I was very young then, around six years old, and of course I did not know how much work was involved. Yet, I knew something drew me to medicine . . . I always loved looking through anatomy books and just bombarded all my doctors with questions!

You need to reach deep down inside yourself and figure out a complete answer with an angle that will make you stand out. Many great essays don't necessarily have to be about a positive experience. Students have successfully written about how they've faced adversity and conquered it to become a better person. Here are some tips on writing your essay that you should keep in mind:

### Be original and innovative

Remember that just as the clubs and activities you're involved in set you apart from other applicants, your essay does the same in a different way. You have more control over the essay in your application than you do over any other part of the process. It is completely your own work, and make sure you are proud of it.

### Be aware of your tone

The tone of your essays is very important. Be true to yourself. Humor can be a good thing, but do not try to be funny if you are by nature a serious person. Readers of your essay may be able to detect a fake tone in your writing.

Remember that anything you write in your essay will be a reflection on you. You don't want to lie to them, and be careful with sensitive topics such as death and controversial issues. If you write something inflammatory, it probably won't help you, and it might even hurt. Use your good judgement.

### Answer the question

It may be tempting to digress, but you should be careful not to go off on tangents. In fact, the first thing you should do is figure out exactly what you are being asked, and make an outline that addresses every part of the question. This is especially important if the question is asking for more than one thing. If you can't follow directions, then you certainly can't handle medical school.

### Use good organization

Make sure you have a central theme and that your essay is coherent and logical. You will want to make sure your ideas flow freely and that they are easy to read. Keep in mind that admissions officials read several hundred essays a week, and they may only spend a few minutes on each one. They can do this by looking for main ideas until they get an overall feeling for the essay. You will want to make their job as easy as possible.

## Sample essay 1

Here is an example of a successful essay written by Constantina Aprilakis from Georgetown University. The assignment was to write about a significant experience:

> *I will never forget the disbelief I experienced when my mother gently explained that my grandmother had lymphoma. It was as though I was being drained of all feeling. I walked back to my room silently, unable to accept that my grandmother had cancer.*
>
> *The months that followed left me void of emotion, unable to release the tears that were building up inside. I found it difficult to visit my grandmother in the hospital. At times, the treatments left her so weak that she could barely utter a greeting when she saw me. Other times, my grandmother suffered from hallucinations, and did not even know that I was there. Each time I visited, I lingered by my grandmother's bed and waited for her to make the sign of the cross over my face. This was something she had done every night since I was a baby. However, during the weeks that the effects of chemotherapy ravaged her body, my grandmother was simply not conscious enough of her surroundings to remember this meaningful act. After every visit, I would sadly give my grandmother one last kiss goodbye. Then I would do the sign of the cross over her head.*
>
> *Night after night, my grandmother battled on, surprising us with her faith and determination. Eventually, my mother was able to bring her mother home. Slowly, the fire reappeared in my grandmother's eyes and the color came back to her cheeks. This shocked the doctors, who had not thought that she would be able to overcome her illness. They warned us not to get excited too quickly. Honestly, I could barely believe the good news. Then, one night I received all of the validation I needed. I had just*

*kissed my grandmother goodnight when she raised her hand and did the sign of the cross over my face. I hurried to my room, overcome with emotion. Suddenly, all of the tears that I had refused to shed poured out. It was the most profoundly moving moment of my life.*

*The doctors' warnings still troubled me. I wondered if my grandmother's health was just an illusion I needed to cling to. What if remission was simply the eye of an unrelenting storm? Then, one day, I just stopped worrying. I decided to enjoy each moment with my grandmother. I realized that no matter what the future would bring, my grandmother had already triumphed. She fought against cancer—and won. In doing so, my grandmother taught me that hope and strength are weapons from within, and miracles really can happen. I learned that as long as I live my life with faith and courage, I could face any hardship.*

*"The best advice I could offer to a student writing a college essay is this: never lie. Always tell a true story. There are two reasons for this. The first is obvious. Lies can come back to haunt you. The second reason is a little more hidden. The thing is, the one thing that makes a college essay outstanding is underlying human emotion. A simple, true story that is moving in its naked honesty is far more interesting than a tale of some fabricated adventure."*

## Sample essay 2

### How I Plan To Make My Mark In Society
### By Hayley Griffin Teich

*For as long as I can remember, my grandfather has been telling me a story about my mother. When she was only a few months old, she became extremely dehydrated and was nearing death as he rushed her to the hospital. After examining her, the pediatrician told my grandfather that he did not think she would live through the night. A young intern, who happened to be at the hospital that night, silently took the baby out of my grandfather's arms and disappeared into another room. The next morning, my grandfather was told that his child would be all right. He later found out that that intern had stayed up all night in an effort to save my mother's life. This young man eventually became a friend of the family and attended many of my mother's birthday parties to celebrate the years that he had helped make possible.*

*This story had a significant impact on me, even as a young girl, because I understood that by saving my mother's life, this intern had unknowingly saved my life as well. It was then that I fully realized the power of medicine. Doctors are capable of touching so many lives. They can truly make a difference in the world. By entering medicine, it is my hope that I can in some way repay the intern who helped my mother. I will follow my dream of helping people and aiding generations to come. Perhaps I, too, will inspire a young child to become a doctor.*

## Your résumé

Résumés are a little easier to construct than essays, but they should not be taken lightly. An admissions official will notice a good résumé right away. It should be eye-catching, not an eyesore.

There are usually two extremes to avoid when constructing your résumé. You don't want to go overboard by listing every imaginable activity you've participated in during your past four years. This could take attention away from an activity that has special significance. On the other hand, you don't want to be overly humble and not mention a CPR class you took or your hospital internship because you think everyone applying to accelerated programs has the same types of things. This would be a mistake.

**Biographical Information you will want to include:**
- List of academic honors
- Extra-curricular activities
- Volunteer experience
- Community service

- Employment
- Medical related activities
- Published papers or research (include a copy)

## Essay and résumé tips

- Brainstorm first.
- Go through multiple drafts.
- Take breaks during writing to check over what you have already written.
- Make sure that your first paragraph gives a good introduction to the paper and that the last paragraph is a conclusion.
- Watch your grammar and spelling.
- Have someone else read your essay and tell you if they think it flows well.
- Let a teacher do a final read for you.
- Anything written on a separate sheet of paper should be typed.
- Include a photo of yourself with your résumé.
- Do a final check to make sure you include everything with the application that is asked for.

# CHAPTER 8

## Letters of Recommendation

*"Many a man's reputation would not know his character if they met on the street."*
—Elbert Hubbard

*"I wish they would only take me as I am."*
—Vincent Van Gogh

Letters of recommendation can easily be the most underestimated part of the application process. Unless you are an incredible applicant, you will probably not be accepted without killer recommendations.

### Why are recommendations important?

You know that you are awesome, but how do you let admissions know that? Well, you could break into their homes while they are sleeping and whisper subliminal messages into their ears. Or you could pay someone to sky-write above the front lawn of the medical school that you "rule." If you are not this daring, however, you can just try just *telling* them how awesome you are, either on your application or during your interviews. This may seem quite obnoxious though, and, well, that's just not going to work.

So what can you do? Your résumé may be impressive, but it probably won't capture your true essence. The answer is simple: You need to have *someone else* tell them how awesome you are. No, not your mom! We are talking about your teachers. Not only are these educated, respected adults, but they've dealt with enough students to know which type can succeed in college and which type is destined to end up flipping burgers. Also, they've spent an entire year or more with you. In other words, what a teacher has to say about you will usually be taken seriously.

### Who should I ask?

After GPA, standardized test scores, and activities, letters of recommendation are what admissions officials use in their deliberative process. There are both good sources and bad sources for recommendation letters. Admissions officials read several similar letters, and you want to be sure that yours sets you aside from the many other applicants. Hence, the best letters come from individuals that know you very well and that have worked with you on an intimate level. Try and obtain letters from various disciplines, not just science.

Good sources:

· Teachers you have worked with and who know you well
· High school counselor
· Research internship instructor
· Community service manager
· Employer
· Doctors that you have worked with in a hospital setting

These are good sources because they are objective. An evaluation from these sources will be fair and impartial. Admissions officials are more likely to give credence to these sources, which reveal the real "you."

Bad sources:

· Family, friends, relatives
· Famous people who you are acquaintances with

These are bad sources because they are heavily biased. Admissions officials will know that these individuals already think positively of you, despite any drawbacks you might have. In addition, it can be assumed these sources would embellish and exaggerate the good qualities that you have.

**Why would a teacher write a good recommendation for me?**
Teachers are usually good intentioned people and should want the best for their students. They realize that it is their responsibility to write recommendations, though some may be more generous about it than others. Certain teachers love writing, and they look forward to that time of the year. On the other hand, some teachers may be very busy and hope that they are asked to write very few recommendations.

You should ask older students which teachers are known for writing touching recommendations. If a teacher likes you, they'll write you a recommendation. If you have impressed them, they'll write you a *good* one.

**How do I know if a teacher will give me a good recommendation?**
We've told you how important it is to have good recommendations, and we've shown you what it takes for a recommendation to be good. The only problem, though, is that you don't write your own recommendations. You do, however, get to choose which recommendations you send, as long as you don't waive your right to do so.

Since you will apply to more than one school, you will need to have the recommendation in your view to photocopy it anyway, so make sure your teachers don't send them directly out. If you ask for more recommendations than you need, then you will be able to choose your favorites and increase your chances of acceptance. Be careful, though, because teachers talk, and if they found out that you've wasted their time, it could mean trouble. In some cases, such as letters of recommendation for medical school, it may be in your best interest to waive your right to view your letters. Use good judgement in teacher selection if you decide this is the case.

## Types of recommendations

Recommendations are not just a list of your accomplishments. Admissions will not want to see a repeat of your transcript. The purpose of a recommendation is to show admissions the qualities that you haven't already shown them. These are qualities that you will not be able to express in other parts of your application.

**Good recommendation**

Many teachers have a standard form letter that they use repeatedly. Their letters can be recognized because everything that they say is something that they really could have said about anyone. In order for a recommendation to be taken seriously it will have to have specific anecdotes that could only refer to you.

> *I had a biology and physics teacher who I spent a lot of time with, and they wrote me great letters. I think those letters are what put me over the edge.*
>
> *Jason Yanofski*

Characteristics of a good recommendation:

- Summarizes you as a individual very succinctly
- Does not restate obvious facts that officials know about (i.e. GPA, standardized test scores, activities)
- Shows your strengths and ability to overcome adversity
- Comes from a reliable, objective source
- Communicates intangibles that can't be conveyed from other sources
- Distinguishes you positively from others in the applicant pool
- Reveals your desire and ability to be a good doctor

## Generic recommendation

Generic recommendations, though saying positive things about you, may actually hurt you. If teachers don't have anything good to say about you, then they won't. That doesn't meant they'd send out a blank piece of paper, but there are many phrases so cliché that it will become obvious to admissions that this teacher doesn't really care much for you.

For instance, if a teacher says that you are one of her better students, that implies that you are not one of her best students, because if you were, she would have said that. You will not be helped by any recommendation that implies you are anything less than the best.

## Negative recommendation

A negative recommendation is one that actually says something bad about you. If you receive a negative recommendation, there is nothing that can save you. This applies to any case where a recommendation is needed. It is possible to avoid this if you read your recommendations before you allow them to be sent out.

> *A friend of mine had impressive statistics but still was not accepted into any of the schools that she applied to. She was very smart, but somewhat whiny and pretentious. Some of her teachers, who she thought were her friends, had some bad feelings towards her and were just waiting to get them down on paper.*
>
> *Cindy Hewitt*

# Tips

## Provide a résumé

It's a good idea to give the teacher a list of activities that you have participated in and your accomplishments. They can use this when they write their recommendation.

### Thank you note

When you are done, make sure that you thank your teacher either in person or by a letter. Of course this won't actually affect you because you already have the letter, but that's etiquette.

### Tell your teacher about accelerated medical programs

There are few reasons why telling your teachers about the program that you are applying to may be good strategy. First, the fact that you would apply to such programs is pretty ambitious, and it shows dedication and focus. Reminding your teachers that you have these qualities couldn't be timelier.

Also, the fact that these programs are highly competitive may persuade your teachers to write you more impressive recommendations because they will know that you really need them. Not only that, but your teacher may somewhat specialize the recommendation to focus on your features that admissions will be most looking for, such as work ethic and leadership abilities.

A final reason for talking about the program is simply that it is an easy way to have a pleasant conversation with your teacher before they write the recommendation. You will want to take any chance you can to get on their good side.

## Sample recommendations

Here are some sample recommendations. See if you can recognize all the traits that they bring out in the student. These writers are passionate in their letters, and admissions will not ignore that.

### Recommendation 1

Let's take a look the opening of this first recommendation written by West Orange High School AP biology teacher, Georgina Hatziemanuel. In the opening, it can be seen right away that the teacher has spent time on this letter, and she clearly makes an effort to set the student apart from other applicants. Between the opening and the closing (not shown here), she goes into detail about her experiences working with him in the classroom and on research over the summer.

Opening:

> *Dear Admissions Officer:*
>
> *What makes Jason Yanofski special and different from other students? In many ways, Jason is a pathfinder, not a pathfollower. He thinks. He ponders. He is extraordinarily quick to learn and to discern. Throughout the AP Biology course that he took with me last year, he listened and asked important and insightful questions which usually began with . . . "What if . . . ?" or "Could it be that . . . ?" or "What I wonder about is . . . " He not only earned an A in the course, he earned a score of 5 on the AP exam.*

Closing:

> *When compared with other college-bound students whom I have taught, Jason is truly one of the most exceptional. Other AP teachers, who have had or currently have him as their student, agree with this appraisal: Jason is a gifted, motivated learner, who demonstrates a lively imagination, leadership, and commitment. There is no doubt that he will be able to handle the social and intellectual challenges offered at your institution of higher learning. He has the potential to make a difference.*
>
> *Should you require additional information concerning Jason's qualifications as a candidate for admission, please contact me at (___) ___-____*

Notice how this teacher completes her letter. Not only does she say that other teachers would also attest to this student's ability, but she provides her own contact information in case admissions wants to discuss the student further. They are not going to call, but it's a nice touch.

## Recommendation 2

This excerpt from a letter written by Dr. Michael Lawrence makes some very powerful statements. It is a safe bet that this letter significantly contributed to the success of the applicant.

> *Jason demonstrates in all types of responses (lab work, quizzes, tests, and homework) his deep understanding of the conceptual nature of physics, so much so that I believe his abilities as a physics student are unparalleled in my 24 years of physics teaching. For example, Jason regularly makes predictions & explanations that reveal a complete and coherent grasp of the concepts under study. Explanation goes to the very heart of science and, generally, the quality of explanation is an indication of the level of critical thinking. In Jason's case, the level of his explanations is unsurpassed in my experience. Furthermore, Jason is the type of physics student who does not rely on equations; instead, he uses his conceptual understanding of physical situations to derive the equations relevant to that situation; this is most impressive when he does his derivations during a test and the problem involves a situation he has not encountered before (although he does recognize the underlying structural similarities between the problem at hand and previous problems . . . an ability that is characteristic of experts, not students, or novices).*

## Recommendation 3

Notice how a letter of recommendation from an employer can portray characteristics in an applicant that can't necessarily be shown from a teacher.

*To Whom It May Concern:*

*I have had the pleasure of knowing Jason Yanofski for the past three years and have observed his work as a Real Estate assistant to his parents as well as other real estate professionals in my office. Over that period I have been highly impressed with Jason's ability to interact with professional people in an aggressive business environment. Despite his youth, Jason has demonstrated superior and innovative computer skills that have benefited his parents and in many cases our entire office.*

*Jason has shown the ability to impart his knowledge to others and has helped many of my agents become both computer and Internet literate. Jason has conducted regular training classes for my associates and many of them have requested and received private tutoring. On numerous occasions he has assisted them in loading and configuring sophisticated software on their personal computers while also helping them perform certain tasks in the office. Many of our agents have commented very favorably on his patience and leadership ability.*

*I have also been impressed with Jason's work ethic. When Jason is given a job to do there is no question it will be performed promptly and accurately. His parents have come to rely on his computer abilities and creativity, as have several other agents in my office.*

*In closing I would whole-heartedly recommend this fine young man for any position or endeavor he may choose to seek and would personally entrust any task to him.*

# CHAPTER 9

## The Interview

*"Man's main task in life is to give birth to himself, to become what he potentially is. The most important product of his effort is his own personality."*
—Erich Fromm

*"Good questions outrank easy answers."*
—Paul A. Samuelson

Congratulations if you've been called back for an interview. Your paperwork has gotten you this far, and now it's your interviewing skills that are going to get you the spot. It's time to really give them what they are looking for.

At this point, all your numbers are put aside, and you start over with everyone on an equal level. This means that coming into the interview, every applicant who was a valedictorian with a 1600 on his or her SAT has an equal chance with everyone else (according to admissions at the majority of programs).

This is not to say that questions about grades or test scores won't necessarily be brought up again. However, if they've had plenty of time to look at your numbers, and if they were not interested in accepting someone like you, then they wouldn't have called you back at all. You've gotten over one of the biggest hurdles now. So relax, and we'll tell you how to have an awesome interview.

**How many people will get called back for an interview with the medical school?**

A general rule of thumb is that only about twice as many students as the medical school is looking to accept are invited to an interview. Those applicants without superior credentials and high test scores will not be called back. What this means is that about half of the people being interviewed will be offered positions, so don't screw it up now!

**Should I bring my parents?**

Most applicants will bring at least one parent. Hopefully they can provide you with a good support system. You do not want them to seem pushy because it may be observed as a sign that *they* are making the decision for you to participate in the program. Parents should show support for their children's decisions and moderate concern. It is expected that they ask some questions and show a general interest in the program but not be annoying or overbearing.

**Who conducts the interviews?**

Each interview will usually be given one-on-one, and will be about a half-hour long. The norm is that you will have two interviews, one with a medical student and the other with a professional, either an MD or a PhD. The professional interview will generally carry more weight, but it is important for both to go well.

*My student interview was very unorthodox to say the least. He told me that if could beat him at chess, he would write a positive evaluation. I thought it was a joke, until he magically pulled out a chessboard from beneath the table. Luckily, a half hour later, it was checkmate . . .*

*Ashish Raju*

### What are they really looking for?

On many previous occasions, we've talked about the qualities that you are trying to prove. Your interview is your last and most important opportunity to do this! To review, you are looking to convey aspects of your character such as dedication, motivation, endurance, leadership, intelligence, organization, maturity, and a love of helping people and learning about medicine.

## The big day

### When will my interview be?

You will be given a specific date for your interview. You can request a change if it isn't possible to be there on that day.

### What should I bring?

Bring any necessary paperwork, a pad and pencil, and maybe a drink or sucking candy (in case your throat gets dry).

### The waiting room

When you arrive, you will probably be told to wait in a room with a handful of other hopefuls. You can look around and talk to some of the other applicants, but don't take anything that they say too seriously. There are likely to be some people there who think quite highly of themselves to say the least. Their cocky attitude may be somewhat justified by their résumé, but don't get intimidated. That attitude is likely to hurt them in the end.

You shouldn't be monitored in the waiting room, but be on your best behavior just in case you are assessed. Someone from admissions should present you with information about the school, and you will get to hear from current students in the program.

### The tour

You will be given a tour of the medical school, and your guide will probably tell you that you will not be judged during that time. This can be a great chance to ask him any questions about admissions or the interviews. If you know who your interviewers will be, find out what qualities those individuals in particular look for.

You can ask your guide general questions about the school and quality of life. Remember that you may be spending four years of your life there. You should have plenty of time to ask these questions to people throughout the day, so enjoy the tour. Be observant and decide if you like what you see.

### Between interviews

You've finished one interview, and you've got one more to go. If things didn't go well, don't sweat it. You may have made a better impression than you think. You've made the trip and have taken a day off from school; don't just give up.

Clear your mind, and start fresh with your second interview. Looking around, you'll be able to get a feel of how everyone else did. Don't be surprised to find someone crying to his parents! Between interviews, you may be served lunch or have a break during which you can leave the building.

> *After I finished my first interview, I came back to the waiting room where a student was talking with the other applicants. Everyone was asking her intelligent questions, and I just ignored her, thinking about the interview I just came from. It turned out that my next interview was with her, and I regretted my earlier reticence.*
>
> Amy Silverman

### Afterwards

Think about anything that may have gone wrong, and use it as a learning experience for your next interview. Send a thank you note back to the interviewer within a week of the interview. If you can cite something interesting that you talked about, that would put you in a good light.

## Preparation

Generally, the format of the interview will be simple: the interviewer asks you questions and you answer them. Because of this, the best way to prepare for your interview is to anticipate the types of questions that you may be asked so that you can answer them confidently. Hesitation is a bad sign, and inability to answer a question could be the end of you.

You should be prepared with at least basic answers to standard questions. There are many other categories of questions that you should be aware of, even though it will be impossible to predict the specific non-standard ones. These include questions about current events and ethical issues.

## Questions

The following sections will tell you everything you'll want to know about what you will be asked during your interview. The questions are broken down by category.

### Standard questions

The first question that you may be asked is why you want to be a doctor. It would be wise to have some sort of an answer to this question prepared beforehand, but you do not want it to look rehearsed. You can focus on the intellectual challenge, the idea of helping people, or the fact that you will spend your whole life learning. Things not to talk about include money, prestige, and hot babes. John Kuruc told us:

> *I had an interviewer who looked like a sweet, old lady. She asked why I wanted to be a doctor and was not satisfied with my answer. She kept asking why to everything I said, and eventually I broke down and told her that it was a very difficult question to answer. The interview ended with her telling me, 'Don't worry, I'm sure you'll get in somewhere.'*

It is very important to show that you are making your own decisions and not that your parents are pressuring you into the field. In fact, it is likely that they will be looking for signs of this. Any indicators of disinterest or insecurity will ruin all your chances. If you are not certain that you want to go to medical school, you probably shouldn't be applying for these programs. Either way, you definitely do *not* want to let your interviewer on to this information. They are only looking for dedicated people who are going to make it all the way.

The next question that you will be asked is: "Why are you interested in an accelerated route?" The best way to answer is by saying something that demonstrates your dedication to the medical field. Express that you couldn't see yourself doing anything else and that you are aware how competitive it is to get into medical school. Tell them that with this guarantee, you feel you would have the opportunity to concentrate more on your liberal arts education, a double major, or some other outside interests. If you are asked what you would do if you were not accepted to a program, you have to remain committed to the medical field in your answer.

Try to grasp the interviewer's attitude about programs. They may be against them. If you sense this to be the case, and you are applying to a seven or eight-year program, you may want to express that you feel six-year programs are too short and that you also value your undergraduate experience.

Another question that you should be expecting is "What kind of doctor do you want to be?" This question is best answered with honesty. If you know that you want to be an orthopedic surgeon because you hurt your knee playing basketball when you were young and admired the doctor who operated on you, that is a good reason.

Stay flexible because it may actually be a turn-off that you are so decided about a specific field without exploring your options. It isn't necessarily a bad thing to say that you are unsure about your residency field. You are young and you have a long way to go before making decisions like these. Your final years of medical school, when you go through your rotations, will really broaden your outlook. If you answer in this manner, it is a good idea to at least be able to list a few fields that interest you and why.

No matter where you are, expect to be asked why you are interested in that particular school/program. Honesty is again the best policy, unless they are a back-up school. Then the best policy is bending the truth. If the case is that you picked it randomly and just wanted to apply to a lot of schools, then you had better think of a reason that you would want to go there.

It is always important to take every school seriously if you want them to take *you* seriously, no matter how strong an applicant you may think you are. This question will allow you to demonstrate your knowledge of the school and show that you have prepared for the interview. So read up on the school and city. Pay particular attention to things that make the school unique.

### Personal questions

Personal questions can be very hard to answer for some people, especially if they are unexpected. It would help to have a few anecdotes in your mind that you'd be able to apply to a variety of different questions that ask you to cite a specific type of experience. For example, if you volunteered as an EMT, you could use that experience to talk about accomplishments, fears, struggles, dedication, volunteerism, etc.

Here is a list of some questions you are likely to see. Remember that a creative question can be answered creatively. Wit, when appropriate, is a very positive thing.

- Who is your best friend and why?
- What was the hardest thing you ever did?
- Tell me about yourself.
- What are your hobbies?
- When was the last time that you helped somebody?
- Tell me something that you are passionate about.

- Where do you see yourself in ten years? Twenty?
- What is your favorite academic subject and why?
- What was the last book that you've read?
- Do you have any major regrets?
- What are your strengths and weaknesses?
- What would you do with a million dollars?

## Questions about your application

The interviewer will almost always have your application in front of them, and they may or may not have recently read over it. Either way, anything that you wrote down is fair game. If something particular stands out, you may be asked about it. This includes your essays, course schedule, grades, activities, and hobbies.

> *One interviewer noticed that I had put humor on my list*
> *of hobbies. He asked me what my favorite television show was,*
> *and I told him Seinfeld. He then went on a five-minute rant*
> *about how much he hated that show.*
>
> *Jason Yanofski*

## Current events and ethics

If you go on a few interviews, without a doubt, you will be asked at least one hypothetical about a controversial issue. You should be aware of current events and issues, especially, but not limited to the field of medicine. Besides newspapers, the best way to stay abreast of these issues is by watching news media (CNN, Today, Good Morning America, The Early Show).

Most of these questions will not have right or wrong answers but are only asked to test your thinking. Don't make a radical stand, but feel free to stand by your answer as long as you can back it up with some kind of logical argument. Here is a list of possible topics:

- abortion and birth control
- genetic testing
- cloning

- euthanasia
- HIV/AIDS
- health care
- drugs
- capital punishment
- the presidency
- confidentiality
- organ donation
- the elderly
- the homeless

Examples of ethical scenario questions:

- What would you do if a man came to you in need of an operation but could not afford to pay for it?
- What would you do if a fourteen-year-old girl came into your office and wanted to have an abortion?
- What do you think is the biggest risk of cloning?

**Prepare a question of your own**
The only question that you can be sure they will ask is whether or not you have any questions of your own; take advantage of this. Think of a smart question to ask that will also show something about your personality. For instance, you might ask about getting involved in volunteer organizations or the quality of their research centers. Remember that you are expected to do research on the school, but you are by no means expected to know everything.

## Tips

### Dress
First impressions are important, and your interviewer will see you before he hears you. Your appearance is more likely to hurt you than help you, so dress conservatively in a suit, blazer, or dress, and shine your shoes. No jeans, sneakers, or loud ties! Comb your

hair, use deodorant, and brush the poppy seeds out of your teeth after breakfast. Dan from New Jersey says, "The more professional you look, the more professional you'll feel."

**Body language**
Use eye contact when appropriate. Avoid too much unnecessary movement, and sit with good posture.

**Attitude**
- Start the interview with a firm handshake. If he doesn't initiate this, you should.
- Don't be intimidated by the personality of the interviewer.
- Stand by what you say, but don't argue.
- Maintain an overall positive demeanor.
- Don't talk too fast.
- Don't curse or use slang.
- Be yourself.
- No death threats, no matter how badly it's going!
- If you have a strong point that you want to emphasize, look for an appropriate time, but don't force it.
- Make sure to leave on a positive note, and thank the interviewer.

# CHAPTER 10

## Rejection and Acceptance

*"I don't know the key to success, but the key to
failure is to try to please everyone."*
—Bill Cosby

*"Defeat is not the worst of failures.
Not to have tried is the true failure."*
—George E. Woodberry

You've made it through the entire process, and you've done everything we've told you – hopefully! Some of you will be accepted to
multiple programs, but unfortunately, others won't even get an
interview. It is likely that the majority of qualified applicants will
land somewhere in between.

### Handling rejection

The notification date for that medical school interview has passed.
You get that small envelope in the mail and your worst fears become a bitter reality. You didn't make it into the program. You
weren't part of the ten percent that were offered admission. Of
course, you may feel inadequate or inferior, but that's not how you
should feel. Before claiming that your life is over and jumping off
a cliff, your first task is to assess why you may not have been accepted.

   Things to analyze are grades, standardized test scores, letters of recommendation, and essays. Did you meet all the deadlines? Did you hold your own on the interview and display your talents? After assessing these pressing questions, it is time to go to your contingency plans. Not getting accepted to an accelerated medical program is not the end of the world. Remember that you can still go to college, excel there, and then apply to medical school.

Just because you weren't accepted to a medical degree program does not mean you will not get into medical school. In fact, the majority of medical school applicants aren't even aware of this alternative application in high school. Cry, shout, scream and let it out. Then suck it up and move on. Work harder and channel this defeat into a positive motivation.

### Assessing the situation

Many students apply to several medical programs to increase their chances of getting into one. If you have not made your first choice, consider going to your second or third choice. If you really want to become a doctor, this is your chance to have a guaranteed acceptance. Going to a less popular program may be an attack on your ego, but in the end, the MD is universal, and it doesn't matter where you get it.

If you have been rejected by all the programs, you will have traditional colleges to fall back on. You can always go to college and take classes over the summer to graduate a year earlier. Once again, going to college and then applying to medical school will allow you to strengthen your academic record and fix whatever prevented you from getting into medical schools directly from high school.

Once you have been rejected from a program, you cannot re-apply. You can forget about programs that are geared for high school students, because you are not going to be a high school student for much longer. You can, however, still try to accelerate through college or look for programs for college students that allow early acceptance into medical school.

### Learning from rejection

Rejection is a valuable learning experience. By applying to a program, hopefully you now know what it takes get into medical school. You have been able to assess the competition you will face later in your college career. You have realized your strengths and weaknesses. You have not lost anything by applying. You have only gained valuable knowledge, and you will be a few steps ahead of the competition when you apply again from college.

You didn't necessarily do anything wrong, but it's possible that due to no fault of your own, you just didn't make the cut, and you are not alone. There are hundreds of highly qualified students who are not accepted to accelerated medical programs. Once again, you must remember that there are limited seats and not everyone can be absorbed by the system. That must be understood with medical school applications in general. Hard work, high grades, and achievement do not always guarantee success. Unfortunately, this is true in general, not just when applying to medical school.

## Applying traditionally

If you are as sure about medicine as you think you are, then you won't give up just yet. You'll go to college, take your MCAT, do research, get involved on campus, volunteer, intern, and then apply traditionally. There are many books on the market about applying traditionally. Unlike applying to programs, if you are rejected from medical schools after graduating college, you can wait a year to build up your application and then reapply. But, after a few years, it's usually time to throw in the towel and move on.

### Foreign medical school

Are foreign medical schools a viable alternative or are they just applications for heartache? Many students who cannot get into medical school traditionally will eventually look to foreign medical schools for the sole purpose of attaining an MD. Please note that we are *not* referring to students from other countries that come to practice medicine in the US. We are talking about US citizens, who attend foreign medical school. Some students also bypass college and apply to these programs after high school. They think this is a way of making their own "accelerated medical program."

We strongly advise against this option. There are several risks you take in applying and attending a foreign medical school. Many students who pursue this option are the ones who don't have what it takes to make it into medical schools in the United States by the traditional method but nevertheless want to become a doctor at any cost.

A foreign medical school has several disadvantages. Most foreign medical schools exist for that particular country and operate for the citizens of that country. The ones that accept foreigners from the US and elsewhere are usually institutions interested most in making money. Such "for profit" institutions have poor facilities. The instruction by the poorly educated staff does not adequately cover the essential curriculum that a doctor needs to carry out his duty in the United States. Several students we have met face linguistic problems communicating with patients in a foreign land. As a result, these medical students do not receive proper clinical and field training.

Many of the students that go abroad to study medicine do not end up practicing in the US. In addition, obtaining a residency position in the US is near impossible especially in the more desired and hence competitive fields such as neurology or ophthalmology. The few students that are admitted from foreign schools are placed in poor residency programs with understaffed urban hospitals. The US graduates usually receive the better positions.

Foreign students must also pass several tests such as the Foreign Medical Graduate Examination in the Medical Sciences (FMGEMS) before being allowed to practice in the US. Several students taking these tests do very poorly and do not pass. In fact, many students who go to these abroad programs have trouble completing medical school in the prescribed years. We have heard of students who have repeated the first year of medical school two or three times! Students also reportedly do poorly on the USMLE parts one and two. The USMLE part one is vital to obtaining a good residency position. Programs for US citizens wishing to pursue a medical degree exist in countries from Mexico to India. However, as you can see, they are very risky and very expensive. Many of these programs require hefty endowments and service in an underrepresented third world nation. Not only that, but after all the travel expenses, phone bills, and other financial burdens, you have a very expensive medical degree without a guarantee that you will be able to work in the US. Leaving family and friends for many years in pursuit of a degree is a difficult choice. Is it one you are willing to make?

Given recent legislation by Congress to limit residency positions to US doctors, these programs are placed in a vicarious position. Use your own good judgement as to whether these foreign medical school programs are right for you.

## Acceptance

Through a mixture of hard work, perseverance, and little help from lady luck, you have made it into a medical program. Congratulations! We hope we were able to help. Jump for joy and call your friends and relatives. It's your time to shine. Don't relax just yet though. This is only another milestone on your road to becoming a full-fledged physician. You still have a long and rough road ahead of you. However, that conditionally guaranteed admission to medical school should be a nice motivating factor to guide you along.

### What do I do now?

You may have one program acceptance or multiple, but you probably have some tempting non-program offers, as well. It's time now to go back to Chapter Two, and decide if accelerated medical programs are really for you. The decision is always yours, but once you give up your acceptance to a program, you can never get it back.

> *I was offered acceptances at Brown, Dartmouth, Cornell, and Yale. The thought of attending an Ivy school did cross my mind. However, seeing myself as a physician helped me accept Lehigh's 6-year BA/MD program. My peers questioned my decision to forsake such highly reputed schools. My counselor even frowned upon my decision to reject Yale. However, looking back on that decision, it is the wisest decision I have made to date. I would make the same decision again and recommend others with similar circumstances to do the same.*
>
> *Ashish Raju*

Things to consider when choosing a program are distance from home, financial aid, school reputation, personal preference, etc. How badly you want that medical degree is usually the factor that allows accelerated medical students to give up their Ivy requests. After matriculation to a program, many don't even give Ivy schools a second look. Why should they? They're focused on medical school now.

## Getting to know the school
If you haven't visited the campus of the school, now is a good time. Go to the open house of the college you have been accepted to. If the medical school and the college share the same campus, you can also visit the medical school. You might have already visited the medical school during your interview process.

Now is a good time to meet friends and possible future roommates. You can decide where on campus you would like to live and what to bring to college. Knowing what to expect is half the battle. Roaming around the campus during your free time will help you get acquainted, and you will be better off when the first day of classes comes around.

## Networking

After being accepted to a medical program, it is a good idea to get into contact with your new advisor. You can discuss what classes to take your first semester and how to prepare yourself for college life. A face to face meeting might also be worthwhile. You might already have a few phone numbers of current students enrolled in the program. Contact these students and ask them about college life and classes as well. The advice from experience of older students will help you avoid unnecessary trouble in your college career.

Finally, you may want to contact fellow program students over the summer. You will be spending a few years with these people. It wouldn't hurt to get an early start. Be active and not passive when it comes to getting things done. You will go farther in college and in life with this attitude.

## Starting from scratch

A harsh reality is that the awards and accolades that students have amassed in high school are history once they enter college. Your 4.0 GPA and 1400 SAT score don't carry over into your college records, and you have to start anew. Don't be discouraged by this.

Your laurels and achievements have gotten you this far and into an accelerated program. Now it is time to further develop your talent, skill, and personality to become a great doctor. Your fellow colleagues are exceptional students with some achievements that even make you stare in awe. But just remember that now you're all starting from the same place and headed in the same direction, towards medical school. Always stay focused on the present and the future, never on the past.

# UNIT IV

## Life of a pre-med?

# CHAPTER 11

## Getting Ready for College

*"It is good to have an end to journey toward,*
*but it is the journey that matters in the end."*
—Ursula K. LeGuin

*"I may not have gone where I intended to go, but*
*I think I have ended up where I intended to be."*
—Douglas Adams

Whether or not you have been accepted to a medical program, you must still get ready for college. You may have friends, siblings, or relatives who have already gone off to college. However, until you go off yourself, it is simply an intangible concept. Being away from home, greater freedom, new friends, tougher courses, and new responsibilities are few of the new things you will encounter as a college student. Nevertheless, here's some advice to keep in mind while you pack your bags and join the millions of students out there behind the walls of academia.

## A new way of thinking

You will quickly undergo a metamorphosis upon entering college. In high school, you spent much time wondering whether or not you would be socially accepted. You spent hours worrying if your clothes were in style and if your friends thought well of you. In high school, you hung out at the mall. In college, you hang out in the quad.

You will be surprised to find out in college that no one really cares what you are wearing, what you eat, or even what you look like for that matter. In college, there is room for diversified personalities and backgrounds. People are more mature and accepting of others. In high school, it may have taken you months to develop a strong friendship with someone. Once entering college, you will confide in your roommate within hours.

Many think this is because in college you literally eat, sleep, and live with your friends. It is pretty hard to not develop strong ties with people. You should expect such openness and maturity. College prepares you for the world after education and the workforce. It's time to grow up! Sachin Ashok Mehta says, "In high school, one makes ideas safe for students. In college, one makes students safe for ideas."

## Packing

Before you load up your worldly possessions into ten suitcases and head off to college, you should really stop and think about what you really need. Remember, all the stuff you take to college, you'll have to live around or in. So be strategic in what you bring.

### Clothes

In terms of clothes, bring whatever you usually wear. The ubiquitous jeans and T-shirt will get you far in college life. Many students usually take clothes in shifts, fall/winter clothes and spring/summer clothes. That way, you will have more room to store other necessities. Unfortunately, if you travel to school in another state many miles away, you may as well take the clothes that you need for the entire school year. One student told us to "pack enough underwear to last at least two weeks. You will get behind in laundry!"

Shoes are an item that will vary from campus to campus. If

you walk a lot to get to classes or happen to live on a mountain (like at the Lehigh program), consider getting a pair of comfy sneakers and saving those boots for some other occasion.

## Hygiene

Cleanliness is healthiness. You will need your usual toothbrush, toothpaste, and bathroom supplies. A shower caddy is essential if you are in a dorm and have to share a bathroom. This will help you carry your soap, shampoo, conditioner, and other shower supplies to and from the bathroom. Invest in a soap dish so that your soap doesn't melt away, and you should also consider buying a pair of "flip flops" or shower shoes. These are slippers you wear in a common shower. Who knows what's growing on that shower floor? Don't forget your towels, and bring a bathrobe.

*Bring two of all your necessities! For example: toothpaste, soap, deodorant, toothbrush, etc. Once my toothbrush fell into the sink, and I was so disgusted because 25 people used the same sink. I threw out my toothbrush but then realized I didn't have a new one in my room to use so I had to go buy a new one.*

*Neha Desai*

## Computers and electronics

People always want to know whether they should bring a computer or not. If you can afford one and prefer using one in your room, go ahead and bring one. Some students don't mind waiting around to use computers supplied by the university. If you plan on bringing a computer, the next question is whether you should bring a laptop or a desktop.

*I chose to bring a desktop computer to school for several reasons—I knew that the types of classes I was planning on taking did not require a computer in class, desktops are harder to steal, and I get more memory and special features on a desktop as opposed to an equally priced laptop.*

*Hayley G. Teich*

Once again, this is a personal preference. Laptops are easily lost and may be hard to repair. On the other hand, desktops aren't really mobile. Use your discretion. Student Neha Desai gives her opinion:

> *I brought a desktop to school but I think a laptop would be so much better because the desktop takes up way too much room. You should buy anything that would help save space in your closet-like dorm room, so I recommend that you buy a laptop over a desktop.*

Most universities offer super-fast T1 Internet connections that have revolutionized college life. E-mail and Instant Messengers have transformed the way we keep in touch and our relationships. Ethernet cards (3Com, etc.) can be purchased for this option in most university bookstores. Many schools also recommend that you buy your computer from certain retailers for best compatibility.

Bringing a printer is also a good decision unless the university provides LAN (Local Area Network) printers. Even if you are allowed access to a printer on your hall, if dozens of other students have access to the same one, there is no guarantee that it will always be operational. You should find out what your school recommends on all of these issues.

Concerning other electronics, you might also want to bring a TV and VCR depending on how big of a TV aficionado you are. Some students get a TV tuner for their computer so that they can watch TV on their computer. This saves space and also means you have to move one less item to and from college.

Many universities provide phones along with voicemail in their residential services. Contact the university to be sure. If you bring your own stereo and have a roommate, it might be wise to pack a pair of headphones. Finally, do not forget the alarm clock to get you up on those cold mornings for your exciting lectures!

**Packing tips**

- Bring lots of hangars.
- Make sure to pack appropriately for the climate of the environment.
- Pack a small first-aid kit with basic health supplies.
- Take dress shirts and a blazer for formal events or interviews; girls should pack dresses and suits.
- Make a checklist of everything you want to bring so that you don't forget obvious items like underwear or towels.
- In regards to big items (TVs, stereos, etc.), contact your roommate so that you know who is bringing what.
- Anything that you forget, you can always buy when you arrive if you need it right away.

## Roommates

Your first decision is whether to get a single or to live with one or multiple roommates. Singles are generally considered a luxury. However, for your first year, when you won't know many people, having a roommate can make things a lot more comfortable.

You can't pick your family, and in most cases, the same holds true for your roommate. You always hear of horror stories about the roommate from hell. If you are given a survey to fill out that matches you with a roommate, be honest. Don't lie about things such as sleeping habits, smoking, and musical taste, or you will be matched with someone who doesn't suit you.

Another important fact is that your best friends do not always make the best roommates. Surprisingly, many randomly matched people who room together are the ones who end up being close friends. You will quickly realize that you are either a highly tolerant person or someone who needs to live alone.

## Your room

### Desks, chairs, and lamps

Most universities provide desks, chairs, and lamps. Bringing your own furniture may be a hassle not worth enduring. Students do, however, sometimes bring comfortable chairs to work in and their own lamps. Once again, this is your own personal preference. If your bottom aches after sitting in a wooden chair for a couple of hours, it's time to get a new chair.

Check with the university as to what kinds of lamps are allowed. Many halogen lamps are not allowed on campus because they pose a potential fire hazard.

### Refrigerator and microwave

Many universities have plans that allow you to rent refrigerators and microwaves for a semester or even a year. Contact your school for more information. If you plan on bringing your own microwave, make sure it is a small compact model that can be placed in a corner.

Consider splitting the cost of these items with your roommate to save money. Make sure all of your appliances are properly wired and meet university standards.

### Storage

After you get to your room, you'll quickly see that space is scarce. In order to optimize your living space, you should consider getting storage crates or "space-saver" under-bed storage containers. Many students decide to "loft" their beds so that they have more room to work. Bookshelves are also good to bring as long as they aren't too big. Some students also bring filing cabinets to store notes and papers.

### Posters

You may find that your dorm room is not exactly appealing to the eye. To cover the drab walls and lighten up your living atmosphere, consider getting a few posters. From favorite sports teams to scant-ily clad women, college students around the world participate in this poster hanging tradition. Consider it part of your passage into collegiate life. Posters also provide an expression of your personal-ity to the visitors of your humble abode.

### Door stuff

In order for your friends to leave you messages on your door, you'll need a dry erase message board with a marker. To make sure you aren't locked out, carry a key chain as well. Doorstops are also an essential item with friends coming and going.

## Other issues

### Nostalgia

Many students suffer from homesickness during the first couple of weeks. To fight these bouts of loneliness, bring pictures of friends and family. A high school yearbook and a couple of small picture albums should suffice.

### Beating the heat and elements

If you happen to live in a dorm that isn't air conditioned, bring a fan to cool yourself off. Many universities allow students with medical ailments (i.e. asthma) to have air conditioners placed in their dorms. That's how some students beat the system. Depend-ing on where your school is, you might want to pack extra stuff such as umbrellas and snow shoes. Here's a tip one student gave us about an extra use for your fan:

> *When hall-mates get annoyingly loud while you're trying to study, turn on your fan high speed and face it towards the wall so you don't get cold. This blocks out all noise, and you are able to study.*

## Safety

Be careful walking around late at night, especially if your school happens to be in a huge city. Use your common sense. Let your roommate or friends know if you are going to be out late and possibly where you might be. Know the numbers of the campus police and health center in case you are faced with an emergency.

## Food

For universities that offer meal plans, pick a meal plan that you are going to follow. If you don't usually eat breakfast, you might consider choosing a limited meal plan (two meals a day, etc.). If you plan on cooking, you might be better off forgoing the meal plan all together or have a limited amount of meals per month.

Aside from ordering that late night pizza and soda, getting non-perishable food is a good idea. The classic "cup of soup" and popcorn help many college students survive the case of the munchies late at night. Packaged drinks and drink mixes (iced tea, etc.) are also compact and useful.

Keep a list of local deliveries and food places in a handy location for when you get sick of cafeteria food. If you have the ability to cook food yourself, be sure to bring the proper utensils as well. Try not to set off the fire alarms while you are at it!

## Laundry

Detergent, fabric softener, bleach, and dryer sheets are your weapons to combat the mound of clothing that piles up in your dorm room at the end of the week. Don't forget the quarters! Some universities allow you to use your ID card to swipe off cash for the laundry and vending machines. If you are having trouble doing your laundry, then take one of those quarters and give mom a call!

# Getting prepared for classes

## Registration

Picking classes is another headache that college students have to endure over and over during their career. (See Chapter 13) Many students avoid those eight AM classes like the plague. You may be better off taking later morning classes and going to a class after lunch. On the other hand, it may be nice to finish your classes by noon, but you may regret it when you start getting up early everyday.

Eventually you'll learn all the tricks. For example if there is a time slot that you are trying to avoid, you may be able to "block" it by signing up for an extra course only given at that time, and then dropping it after your schedule is made.

## Stationary/school supplies

You can buy your usual stationary such as notebooks, loose-leaf, and writing utensils without any problems from the school's bookstore. Stock up on materials because you'll make use of them in some form or another. More specialized equipment such as graphing calculators is important, depending on what classes you are taking. These can always be purchased when you find out that you need them. Also, in order to keep track of your schedule, you should get a calendar or electronic organizer (Handspring, etc.).

## Textbooks

Nothing burns money and empties your wallet as quickly as buying college textbooks. They can range in price anywhere from relatively cheap to $200 plus. There are, however, ways to beat the system. Buy used textbooks early. Find out what classes you are taking and then race everyone else to the bookstore to get your hands on them. A second option is to buy your books from upperclassmen.

There is also competition with university bookstores in the form of online booksellers, one of the largest being ecampus.com. Purchasing books online can save you 10-50% off the retail price. As a college student strapped for cash, this should definitely help a little. Get together with friends and order together to save more money.

After you have used your books, you may also resell them back. Be wary though; you might need that textbook in a later course for reference. In addition, the price you get selling it back may not be fair in terms of what you paid and what condition the book is in. If all else fails, you can always sell it to a freshman for just below asking price!

**Finding everything**
You're going to get lost the first few days of class. It takes time to get acquainted to a college campus. This isn't high school, and you are no longer on top of the food chain. You can always tell the freshmen on the first day of class. They are the ones carrying the maps around with them and look confused.

In order to avoid being late to class or even slight embarrassment, it might be a good idea to walk to your classes a couple of days before they begin. This will help you get better acquainted with your campus and possibly make some new friends. You can memorize the campus map, find others in your classes and follow them, or just go by trial and error. Eventually, you'll get the hang of it.

## Have pride

Be proud of your school and what it stands for. All schools have a deep and rich history. The school you are going to may not be your first choice, but it is where you are now. The last thing you want to do is carry resentment throughout all of your college years. This almost always inevitably shows in your grades and relationships. If you really can't stand your environment, it may be time for you to leave the accelerated program and transfer/apply out. (See Chapter 17)

# CHAPTER 12

## How to Pay

*"A fool and his money are soon parted."*
—Thomas Tusser

*"There's no such thing as a free lunch."*
—Milton Friedman

This chapter was written by financial expert Nihar R. Desai. He tells about his experiences in high school and college, showing us that there are ways to make paying for school easier.

## Introduction

As we enter the new millenium, enjoying success in this world has become more difficult than it has even been. College-level studies are becoming a prerequisite for all jobs. However, with the price of higher education at the level it is, the task has become more daunting than ever. In fact, to get a four-year undergraduate degree from a private institution of higher learning, one should expect to pay well over $100,000.

In the next few pages, I have attempted to outline and explain, in a systematic manner, the various methods by which students can receive financial help as well as defining some of the technical terms that you are likely to encounter in this process. Please note that these are the same sources I have used and they have enabled me to attend a university whose price tag is close to $33,000 for about $10,000.

Before I start explaining the outlining, let me tell the plain and simple truth about financial assistance – the money and the opportunities are out there; you just have to know where to look and what to do. This is my objective in writing this section, to help students help themselves.

## High school scholarships

As a high school student, the opportunities for financial aid are quite simple to find. At most high schools there are officials such as guidance counselors or college counselors. In addition to providing students with information and advice about course schedules and career options, they should have a list of scholarship opportunities.

At my high school, there was a bulletin board full of applications and I would go by every Tuesday and take a copy of every single one. I had nothing to lose, maybe a few minutes filling out the application, so I made sure to fill out every application that I met the requirements for and you should do the same!

Usually, the scholarships offered through the school are set up by alumni, members of the city, and local foundations/organizations for students who have certain career aspirations, played certain sports, or have particular interests.

Be sure to aggressively pursue all of the scholarships that you are eligible for and remember the old lotto phrase, "You can't win if you don't play." Thus, in terms of opportunities offered by the school, I advise you to get to know your counselor if you have not taken the time to already, and apply for everything you can – you have nothing to lose except those outlandish price tags for a college education.

### Local professionals
There are several other options you have while in high school to

get some financial assistance besides the conventional way outlined above. First, go down to your city hall and find a directory
listing all of the various businesses and professionals in your town.
These are usually listed in alphabetical order, i.e. accountants, car-
penters, doctors, real estate, etc. If you know what you are going
to study in college then immediately find that profession within
the book. For example, I am studying to become a physician so I
went through all categories dealing with medicine, i.e. doctor's
offices, hospital committees, private laboratories and pharmacies,
etc.

Once you have located your prospective sources, draft a letter
in which you outline your goals and accomplishments. Also tell
them why you are deserving of their monies and what you intend
on using their assistance for. Be clear and concise and be sure to
offer them a look at your résumé or an interview if that will help
their decision.

To be quite frank, I wrote about 50 letters of this nature (you
just use the draft and change the name each time) and got quite a
bit of money from local professionals. However, do not expect companies or organizations to give you thousands of dollars because
they probably will not. Instead, explain to them that any contribution, whether it be $50, $100, or $500, will be greatly appre-
ciated and properly spent, and that every little bit helps!

Once again, be aggressive; all you have to lose is the ten minutes you spent drafting the letter and the price of the stamp. However, even if you get only one or two positive responses, remember
that you have gained considerably.

### National scholarship lists

A second option one can pursue outside of the high school realm is
to buy a scholarship book from a local bookstore such as Barnes
and Noble. These books cost about $30.00 and literally list thou-
sands upon thousands of funds and foundations that are setup for
prospective students. Many of these have requirements associated
with them, such as career goals, sports interests, ethnic background,
or hobbies.

I applied to many scholarships that dealt with medicine but also those that had golf, classical music, or Asian American background as their requirements. Unlike the local scholarships offered through the school, to win one of *these* scholarships, you will be competing on the national level. Consequently, these scholarships may grant the winners thousands of dollars. Again, my advice here is the same as before, be aggressive! Remember you have nothing to lose (use the same draft you used before; just change the name and address).

When you go through this book you will believe my simplified philosophy – the money is out there, you just have to know where to look and what to do. These books are comprehensive and I encourage you to go through and apply for every scholarship that you meet the requirements for.

Be concise and clear in your initial approach but do not be surprised if they ask you for a copy of your résumé or a personal statement (about 500 words) seeing as these awards are very prestigious.

## Business scholarship funds

The last source of financial assistance while in high school is perhaps the simplest. All you have to do is to ask your parents if their place of work or business has setup a scholarship fund for employees' students. If your parents work for a small business then having a fund for students is probably out of the question, but if they work for a big corporation then it is a likely source of aid.

My father works for the United States Postal Service and my mother works for a bank and both organizations had funds setup to help employees' families with paying for college. These awards are not as large as some others but always remember the old adage, "every little bit helps."

## College scholarships

The four major sources mentioned above are all open to students when they are in high school. The transition from high school and college brings about drastic changes in academics as well as financial aid. There are four major documents that you will become familiar with when you apply for financial aid at the collegiate level:

- Free Application for Federal Student Aid (FAFSA)
- College Scholarship Service Profile (CSS Profile)
- Form 1040 (also 1040A or 1041EZ)—US Individual Income Tax Return
- Form W2

These forms can be somewhat intimidating because they are unfamiliar to you. However, I will attempt to simplify all four of these documents and explain them in the simplest terms possible.

### FAFSA

The Free Application for Federal Student Aid is the document students must file in order to receive assistance from the government. This aid can come in a variety of forms; when people use the words "federal student aid" they mean federal grants (monies you do not have to pay back), loans (which you must pay back), and work study (monies you earn through a job on campus).

It is a very important document not only because it allows students significant financial aid but also because the government uses the information provided to do various calculations which are crucial figures when it comes to paying for your education. Before we engage in an in-depth discussion of the FAFSA, let me first outline all of the various awards you may receive from the government (we will come back to them a little later):

- Federal Pell Grants
- Federal Supplemental Educational Opportunity Grants (FSEOG)

- Federal Subsidized and Unsubsidized Stafford Loans
- Stafford/Ford Federal Direct Subsidized and Unsubsidized Loans
- Federal Perkins Loans
- Federal Work Study
- Title VII and Public Health Act Programs

Your first objective is to get your hands on the application. The conventional paper application can be obtained from the guidance office at your high school or even at the local library. Nowadays, the application can even be obtained via the Internet at www.fafsa.ed.gov. To begin filing the application you will need access to the two very important documents mentioned above, the Form 1040 (or any variant) and the W2.

**Form 1040**

The Form 1040, as your parents will tell you in a depressed voice, is the Federal Income Tax Return. It is filed every year and sent to the Internal Revenue Service (IRS) for processing. The form asks for a wide variety of information but it concentrates on wages, salaries, and other forms of income for the family. With the figures provided in the form, the IRS uses a formula to calculate how much money in taxes you or your family owes to Uncle Sam. Although the Form 1040 is quite complicated, for the purposes of our discussion all you have to understand is that it is a form filed to determine how much money in taxes is owed to the government based on total income.

**Form W2**

The W2 is not a form that you must complete; instead it is simply a statement of your yearly wages and other incomes provided by an employer. In other words, the information on the W2 is usually used to complete many portions of the Form 1040. Once you have obtained the application and have completely filled it out, you can send it via an envelope provided in the application packet to the federal processing center.

### Student aid report

After several weeks, you will receive what is termed the Student Aid Report (SAR). It is usually a series of blue papers, which provide you with information on your eligibility for federal financial aid. In fact, it will explicitly explain which of the above programs you are eligible to receive.

There are two important aspects of the SAR that you should look for. The first is what is called the Estimated Family Contribution (EFC). This will most likely be located on the first page in the upper right corner. The EFC is what the government, after a thorough look at the FAFSA, feels you or your family can contribute to a college education. The other piece of information will explicitly tell you which federal programs you are eligible to receive.

Although you should be happy to receive any assistance from the government the two "best" awards are obviously the grants and secondly any subsidized loans. The grants, which can be either Federal Pell Grants or Federal Supplemental Educational Opportunity Grants (FSEOG) are funds that you will not have to pay back.

Many people do not like to receive loans because they must be paid back with interest, but the subsidized loans do not require you to pay interest until six months after you graduate. Thus, if you pay the entire loan back within six months of graduation, you will only pay back the face value of the loan. The Stafford and the Stafford/Ford loans have limits on how much can be borrowed depending on the year of study. These figures change quite often but they will be given in your SAR if you are deemed eligible. Although this may seem to be time-consuming and frustrating, you are not yet done with Uncle Sam.

At this point, you will have your EFC and a list of any/all funds you will be receiving. However, your EFC is also sent to the colleges and universities where you applied for admission. So the bad news is that you will have to remain sharp and dedicated to your financial aid. The good news is that each of the schools that you applied to will look at your EFC and the government assistance and try to meet your needs even better.

Each school has endowments and assistance from their alumni. These funds are usually given in the form of grants and loans to prospective students. Thus, with the government package and the schools package you will be given the correct amount of financial assistance to meet your EFC. All of the aids mentioned thus far have been based on the EFC calculation determined by a federal processing center and based on your responses given on the FAFSA.

The FAFSA and its EFC are used to provide students with financial assistance through the federal government as well as the respective schools the student applied to. However, it is important to remember that any financial assistance given to the student by the school is based on a federal calculation of the EFC. For public universities, this is the end of complicated forms and dealings with the government.

### Scholarship service profile

If you choose to enroll in a private university, you will be required to file a second form, the College Scholarship Service Profile (CSS Profile) which is created by The College Board. This application is very unique in that only certain schools require it and it is customized for each student. This is also a very important form because it will be used by colleges and universities to provide you financial assistance.

The first step in the CSS Profile procedure is to obtain the preliminary application. Once again you can get the application in paper form from your counselor or you can obtain it via the Internet from The College Board's web site. This is a simple form, mainly asking your name, address, and the names of those universities that you applied to. With this filled out, you then call the Profile Hotline and provide them with the information on the preliminary application.

Once they have the names of universities you applied to that require this financial application, they will send you a customized application. This application is customized solely for your use and is based on the fact that certain schools only want certain pieces of information. Again, you will have to sit down and diligently answer all of the questions on the CSS Profile as requested by the universities you applied to.

Although the use of the CSS Profile seems redundant to many, it is necessary step in the process. In fact, the Profile asks many different questions than were on the FAFSA and they tend to be more detail oriented and focus on other aspects of your financial situation such as equity and property.

Once you have completed the application and sent it to the College Scholarship Service Processing Center you will receive a postcard acknowledging your completed application. Your application goes through the same steps as it went through with the FAFSA in that it goes through a processing center that once again establishes how much you and your family can contribute towards your education. This value will be different from your EFC that was obtained from the FAFSA.

Once again, the contribution value determined through the CSS Profile will be sent to those particular schools that require it and the financial administrators will use it to develop a financial package that meets your needs. This package can include many of the things we have talked about such as grants and loans but you may also see something called work-study on your financial aid offer.

## Work study

The work study award requires you to obtain an on-campus job (library, particular academic department, admissions office, etc) and you are given a paycheck. The financial aid officer assumes that you will use the paycheck to pay for your tuition bills but they leave that decision to you. Thus, the work-study is a unique source of funding because it does not go directly to your education but requires the student to be financially responsible.

### Other scholarships

The last major component of financial aid that I want to discuss is one that I have already mentioned – outside sources and scholarship books. I brought these two sources up when we first began talking about sources for the high school student. However, they can be even more rewarding when you enter the college ranks. Again look for alumni that share your particular career interest or hobby, and apply for as many scholarships as humanly possible.

## Conclusion

In the preceding pages I have attempted to outline the rigorous financial aid procedure as simply, quickly, and clearly as possible. As this section comes to an end, let me reinforce some ideas that I consider fundamental to financial aid success.

First and foremost, develop a solid foundation in the process and pride yourself on knowing what you are talking about. The process and the formulas can be quite intimidating and very complicated. You do not need to know every detail but it is important to know the basics such as the ideas outlined above.

Secondly, be aggressive and pursue all your possible sources and options. I cannot emphasize the lotto motto enough, "You can't win if you don't play." Thirdly, always remember the simple and basic truth about financial aid – the money and the opportunities are out there, you just have to know where to look and what to do. Lastly, although I encourage you to explore all of the different sources I have outlined, be creative and try to find some other places to look for aid. Remember, you have nothing to lose but those daunting college expenses.

I told you that my objective in writing this section was to help students help themselves. I hope that this section is helpful to you, and I wish you the best in your college search and in the financial aid process.

# CHAPTER 13

## Dealing with the Curriculum, Professors, and your Advisor

*"I never let schooling interfere with my education."*
—Mark Twain

*"Advice is like snow; the softer it falls, the longer it dwells upon, and the deeper it sinks into the mind."*
—Samuel Taylor Coleridge

To the surprise of many, accelerated medical programs are not as stressful as people would have you believe. In fact, in most cases, programmers have more free time and enjoy themselves more than traditional pre-meds do. Because programmers have a near-guarantee and know what their requirements are, they don't have to fear new classes and unknown subject areas.

Nevertheless, staying in the program requires careful attention and hard work. In addition, some new rules apply to programmers in ways that you would not expect. Let's examine how you can optimize your time in the program by discussing what you need to know about courses and interactions.

## Classes

Most accelerated medical degree programs have core classes which you're required to take. The usual classes are biology, chemistry (inorganic and organic), mathematics, and physics. These classes prepare you for medical school. All programs will also have elective requirements, and the flexibility you have in choosing these courses will vary by program.

**Using AP credit**

Course selection can be a painstaking task, and having advanced placement (AP) credit means you will need to decide which classes to place out of. As a general rule, any AP credits that will place you out of a humanity or social science are credits that you will want to use. These classes include economics, American history, political science, etc. The reasoning behind this rule is that by coming in with more credits, you will have more leeway with your schedule later on. If you finish your requirements early, then you will be able to take whatever you want after that. It is likely that you may want to take more humanities and social sciences with that time, but it is still strategic to cash in those AP's from the beginning to keep your options open.

In regards to AP science credits, it is your decision whether or not to use them. Most students, if given the opportunity, will place out of introductory chemistry, physics, and biology. On the other hand, some feel that they could use the "review" of the course and receiving some solid A's early on would be a pragmatic move. It is important to set up a cushion for yourself in case of an emergency later on.

The course review may also help if you feel your high school AP courses were not at the same level as college courses. If you start with an advanced course and don't know what's going on, you could be in hot, shark-infested water!

Thus, if the courses you are considering skipping over are prerequisites to harder courses, or if they'll be covered on the MCAT, don't place out unless you feel 100% competent with the material. Since mathematics isn't directly tested, you should place out of introductory calculus if possible. More information about AP tests can be found in Chapter 4. In summation, placing out of college classes benefits you by allowing:

- The required # of credits to graduate to be attained at an earlier time
- You to take more classes that you like or that better prepare you for medical school
- Greater flexibility in your college years and possibility of a double-major

**When to take classes**

Doing well in college is like a game. These are some of the inside tips that will help you score points! Some professors will be better teachers than others, and even though they may be the best and brightest in their respective fields, this does not guarantee that they can teach a classroom of college students. There are several reasons why this may be the case. It may be because they feel uncomfortable talking to a large group of students or that they can't express their ideas in an effective manner for students to learn. Either way, sometimes choosing a course by *who* teaches it is more important than choosing it by content.

The best way to pick classes is to find out as much information as possible. Speak with students who have taken the class before and find out if they recommend it. Since you want to maintain a high science GPA, it is essential that you know the best time to take a class taught by a specific professor. Invariably, there are off-semesters where the class taught is easier than the regular semester, and courses are almost always easier during the summer.

Another good source of information about course selection is your pre-medical advisor. He or she has advised hundreds of students and will most likely know which classes are good and bad for someone like you. A helpful pre-med advisor will ask students for feedback about courses and then relay that information to others, helping them to make well-founded decisions. We'll talk more about your advisor later in this chapter.

Generally, you should try to take all your requirements first, but don't take too many of the same type of course at once. It makes sense to spread out heavy writing, reading, or math intensive courses if you can. Also, your first semester doesn't need to be exceedingly demanding, because you will want time to explore and adjust. It's also nice to start off with an auspiciously strong semester. Again, you will want to set up a nice cushion for yourself. Here a student explains some of his schedule choices:

> *I didn't take genetics last semester because a reliable friend who took it the year before told me that the professor who taught it then was a jerk and failed 40% of the class. Instead, I took an awesome philosophy course about Kant and the categorical imperative. I took it because it was interesting, and it was a good change from organic chemistry and all that biology. Next semester, a different professor is teaching genetics, and I will take it then.*
>
> *Derek Starr*

### Non-science classes

Science courses are not enough to ensure that you will become a good doctor. A doctor should be more than a textbook. They need deliberation and communications skills. While in college, take interesting classes outside the medical field.

Some programs specifically emphasize this diversity. Philosophy, law, and computer science are a few examples of the classes many programmers will take during their program years. Remember, this is a perfect time to enjoy your classes and to take ones that interest you. Once in medical school, opportunities like this will not be possible. Yet, another option for this available semester could be to study abroad or to do an internship.

### Advanced science courses

Finally, if you have met your requirements and have a semester or two to spare, it is highly recommended that you try some high-level medical school courses, such as biochemistry, histology, immunology, and anatomy. Obviously, having a preview of medical school will assist you during your first year.

Your advisor may persuade you to take advanced courses, or she may suggest that you use your available time taking liberal arts classes that you won't be able to take again. Either way is acceptable, but beware: it's not worth taking difficult classes if doing so puts you in a situation where you have a chance of risking your GPA eligibility. It doesn't help to take medical school-type classes if you get kicked out of the program and are not accepted into medical school.

*You* are the best judge to decide if you can handle a specific course or course load. If you have been getting a 4.0 all along with a really tough schedule, then you probably know what you are doing.

However, if your grades are borderline and you are worried about doing poorly in advanced science classes, you may decide to audit them without receiving a grade. The point of taking these classes is to obtain knowledge and to solidify you for the rigors of medical school, not to create more obstacles for yourself.

### The curve

It is important to realize that the way that college classes score your grade is different than how things worked back in high school. Many classes are graded harshly, and the average test grades may be in the 50's or lower. Usually the average score represents a grade of a "C+" or "B-," which means if you scored a low number grade but it was significantly higher than the average, you may have earned an "A."

Don't have a cow over missed points, man! Just find out where you stand and how the class is curved. If you don't understand that everything is relative, your grades will mislead you and you may be surprised when you get your grade report in the mail.

**Class attendance**

College professors won't look after you like your high school teachers did. Some professors will keep attendance, but most won't, especially in large lecture halls. It's very easy to get lazy, especially for those early eight AM classes. Even if you can handle the material from the textbook alone, going to class will allow you to learn what will be stressed on the exams, and you will stay more on top of things.

Of course, if you really are sick, you don't need to force yourself out of bed when you're sure that nothing important is going on in class, and you can get the notes from a friend. If professors start getting ticked off that students aren't showing up, however, they may give surprise quizzes designed to benefit everyone who *did* come to class that day. If you are the type who sometimes goes and sometimes doesn't, then you are definitely playing the odds, and you won't always win.

## Professors

Just because you are in a program does not mean that you should be given any special treatment within the classroom environment, and expecting anything more can lead to trouble. Because of this, if you don't have to, you might not want to mention to a professor that you are in the program.

In addition, while many professors think that program students are the brightest on campus, there are others who dislike programmers for several reasons. These are some of the stereotypes that may follow programmers:

- Programmers take classes only because they are part of their core requirement. Teachers feel that programmers do not have a genuine interest in the class.

- Jealousy can be present because program student may have had it easier than *they* did. Many science professors may have unsuccessfully applied to medical school at some point in their lives.

- Programmers are known to knit-pick for points because they are very grade conscious. Arguing with any faculty, especially a professor, is not fruitful.

- Professors have spent their whole lives dedicated to their field and may feel that programmers are merely learning the minimal amount to get by.

- Adversaries may feel that programmers aren't mature enough to be offered a position in medical school, and want to make things as difficult as possible.

The best advice would be to keep your programmer status on the down low. This may be a problem to those of you with big egos. However, humility is a trait that has great moral worth, and a good doctor is expected to carry this trait in his or her profession. Start working at this during your program years.

When recommendation time rolls around, you will need to ask professors to write letters for you. In order to avoid awkward requests later in your college career, be sure to develop strong relationships with your professors from day one. Ask questions, get involved, and go that extra mile to show professors that you really want to learn and that you do care about the subject matter. In addition, teaming up with professors for research projects and internships always boosts an already illustrious résumé.

If you and a professor just can't see eye to eye on an issue, or you feel you have been treated unfairly, you can always talk to your advisor or the dean. Only do this if absolutely necessary. Things not to do include sending nasty e-mails or voice-mail messages, threatening to sue, or throwing small rodents!

Remember that some professors are great people and will be able to make learning fun, but there are others who are just jerks. Usually their reputations are based on truth, and as stated earlier, choosing the right professor can often be more important than choosing the right course.

## Your advisor

A good advisor is important to the success of your college career whether you are in a program or not. For the most part, advisors are qualified and helpful. Since you are in a program, you will most likely receive a specialized pre-medical advisor. The best way to gauge your advisor is to ask older programmers (upperclassmen) about him or her.

You can also evaluate your advisor on your own. Does she know the latest information on medical college admissions scores, GPA's, financial information, and other related information? Does she offer suggestions as to which classes are better than others? Is she supportive and understanding?

Your program advisor can be your best friend or your worst nightmare. She may have a different attitude toward program students depending upon what school you are at. Ideally, your advisor is supposed to help you with your decisions, but people are not always what you'd like them to be. Here are two generic advisor-types that may put a strain on your college years:

1) One type deals with a lot of traditional pre-meds, seeing what a tough time they're having. She thinks that program students are brats who complain too much and don't know how good they have it.

2) Another type, at a school where students can chose between two-year and three-year curriculums during their undergraduate time, favors students who chose one route over the other.

We don't want to discourage you from working with your advisor. The two of you hopefully will get along great. While your advisor can be a valuable source for information, only make decisions that you feel totally comfortable with because only *you* can fully understand your personal goals.

**Getting in contact**
You should be able to make an appointment to meet with your advisor before each semester to discuss your progress and class selection. There are also other times when you would need to contact with her. If you are having trouble with a professor, thinking about adding or dropping a class, or have any questions about your requirements or the program in general, you should speak with her right away.

Calling and leaving a message or sending e-mail will do the trick for questions that can be answered easily. If you don't get a response within a few days, try again, or be proactive by calling her secretary to set up an appointment.

## Choosing between two and three years

Some accelerated programs are six years in length, and others are seven. At a few programs, you will have the option of choosing how long you want to stay. You may have to make this choice going into it, or you may have no commitment to decide until the very end.

This is a very personal decision. Some cons for staying the third or fourth year include paying for an extra year of school, taking an extra year of classes, and not getting to medical school for another year. The pros of staying longer are the same as those advantages gained by finishing your requirements early:

- Not having to stay summers
- Gaining the chance to take more classes or an additional major
- Having the option of spreading out your classes so that your individual semesters are lighter

- Experiencing an extra year of college to relax and party
- Having another year before taking the MCAT
- Gaining an extra year to mature before facing medical school

## Double majoring

In this piece, Jamie Swanson tells us how staying an extra year has allowed her to double major, among other things:

> *In my heart I know I truly love medicine, but there are some things that I want to try first before I dive into the four hardest years of my life. I have found that I really like writing for the school newspaper, that I will love my sorority sisters forever, and that the best part of college is the social life-like parties, boys, and spring break.*
>
> *But besides taking advantage of sorority life or writing for the paper, staying a third year has a more valuable purpose for me. I also have time to work on a second major in journalism and participate in a yearlong research project. There is a misconception that students will miss out on college if they are in accelerated programs, but that doesn't have to be the case.*
>
> *Many friends of mine have used their extra year to do great things too. They have also pledged or double majored, as well as spending a semester in Washington, becoming a resident advisor, singing in the choir, or enriching their lives in other ways.*
>
> *Even if they are not double majoring, at least they are taking some classes outside of the required science electives. There are other classes besides biology, physics and chemistry. Medical schools usually require non-science electives, so it's obvious that they want students with varied backgrounds.*
>
> *Taking other classes and double majoring can directly help pre-meds in other ways too. Maybe those economic classes will come in handy when it comes time to fill out the loan applications. The public speaking classes will be useful for students when they have to face intimidating attending physicians on their*

*rounds. Hopefully the English and journalism classes will spice up patients' charts and help doctors find the perfect word to describe a patient's symptoms. Even the sociology classes will help when dealing with patients' family problems.*

*I firmly believe that we will all be better doctors for all of this. When pre-med students expand their horizons and broaden their curriculum, they open themselves up to new perspectives. They can also open themselves up to new career paths. There is also a whole world out there for doctors besides just working in hospitals and having a practice.*

*Doctors also work in pharmaceutical companies doing clinical research, as the health reporters on television and newspapers, as teachers at medical schools, even for insurance companies. There really is no limit, except that people usually only see a doctor's career in one way. From a financial standpoint, doctors with special skills and talents have the potential for greater success. They also have the opportunity for the greatest personal happiness.*

*To paraphrase Steve Jobs, even pre-med students need to think outside the box. Many of us were drawn to medicine for that very reason. As doctors we will be faced with challenging problems to solve, and we can best fix them when we apply all of our experiences and knowledge. But if our only knowledge comes from taking the required science classes, we aren't going to be very helpful.*

*So my advice to all pre-med students out there is simple. If you are considering applying to an accelerated program, ask questions about staying a third year and double majoring. You really do get the best of college without the hassle. It might be the only break you get in the grueling journey to your life's dream.*

## Special treatment

Because the program curriculum is generally viewed as very strict and compact, program students are often thought of as exceptional. One student said, "When it comes to getting exempt from certain requirements or requesting a 21 credit semester, saying BA/MD will pretty much allow you to get approval. They trust that these students are smart and can handle a lot."

This special treatment can also work against you. Find out early what special rules you need to follow. Besides the standard GPA and MCAT requirements, you may be prohibited from such things as taking courses pass/fail or transferring credits from other schools. Check with your advisor along the way, so you don't get any surprises at the end when you are ready to go to medical school.

## Summers

After a rough year of classes, the last place that you want to be during your summer is back at school. Going two or three years straight without a break can be intolerable. The good news is that you probably won't need to do this. Eight-year programs definitely won't require summers, seven-year programs may or may not, and six-year programs more than likely will require at least one summer.

Usually, taking a heavy course load during the year or coming in with a lot of classes can put you in a position where you may not need to stay the summer, or at least all of it. Typically the summer is divided into two separate sessions.

Taking classes during the summer isn't that bad. Summer classes are usually easier and more relaxed. Some classes, like organic chemistry, may be significantly more manageable over the summer. Since professors need to cram several months of work into about a six-week period, the classes will be longer and more frequent. Overall, the required material will still be covered during that time.

The Penn State University six-year program requires that student start the summer right after they graduate high school. That's definitely not where you would want to be during that summer, but that's the price you'll need to pay to be at Jefferson Medical College two years later.

# CHAPTER 14

## Study Habits, Tips, and Tricks

*"If you want to test your memory, try to recall what you were worrying about one year ago today."*
—Rotarian

*"The test of a first-rate intelligence is the ability to hold two opposed ideas in mind at the same time and still retain the ability to function."*
—F. Scott Fitzgerald

Whether you are in high school, college, or medical school, effective studying is an asset that future doctors must master. Some students spend 3-4 days studying prior to a test, while others study the night before for only few hours.

A misconception that is held by many students is that good grades are directly proportional to the amount of time you spend studying. If this were the case, everyone could become a doctor if they worked all day and night. The answer lies in the effectiveness of the studying, not the amount of time you put in.

A good solid 4-6 hours spent understanding key concepts and absorbing pertinent information is far more valuable then a whole day spent trying to make sense of notes that seem like they were taken in a foreign language. Learning the proper ways to study effectively will vital to your success at college and in your medical career. Hopefully, this chapter will help you to do just that.

## Typical pre-medical science courses

The following dissection of typical college courses and how to attack them will be useful. Much of the advice given may seem like common knowledge, but reading it in an organized matter will put things into a clearer perspective. Let the crystallization begin!

### Calculus

Calculus for some of us comes faster than for others. Nevertheless, there is no reason why any student cannot eventually solve a problem with proper instruction and patience. Unfortunately, tests are usually timed and the ability to correctly calculate those derivatives and integrate quickly is what gets you A's on exams. The best tip for calculus is to work on problem sets. Do a particular type of problem over and over until it becomes second nature.

For example, if you are having trouble with the chain rule, first, understand the concept behind it. Then apply it in several problems until it becomes automatic. Most importantly, do not ignore weaknesses in any particular area. This is because concepts build upon themselves. This particular property is not exclusive to calculus; it holds true for physics and chemistry as well. Once you master the basic principles of calculus, you should be able to apply them well.

### Chemistry

Chemistry comes in various forms for pre-medical students. You usually start off by learning inorganic and basic principles. Once again, remember to understand general concepts and trends. If you do not understand a particular lesson, don't ignore it. Seek help! Read the chapters from the textbook if you feel that your professor just isn't cutting it for you. If that doesn't work, then ask a peer for help. You will be amazed at how easily it is to understand concepts when it comes out of your friend's mouth.

The most dreaded chemistry course is without a doubt organic chemistry, known sometimes as "orgo." I am sure you have heard horror stories of people struggling with orgo. Once again, we see that understanding large concepts and applying them in specific settings is what determines success. Lehigh organic chemistry professor and department chair, Keith J. Schray gives us "the real skinny."

- *This is a very tough course, for some of you the toughest course you will take at college. Whoa, now there's news! But read on.*
- *You've heard it is all memorization. NOT TRUE! If you do not yet grasp mechanisms, then you must start learning them and never quit. There is no other way to deal with the volume of material. You cannot memorize very much gibberish and if you don't understand it, then it is gibberish. Do you have to memorize? Sure, but understand it first!*
- *You can't learn it all! So, create condensed notes that you can master. Prioritize! Learn well the first set of most important information. Then go to the second level and learn that. Organize and Prioritize.*
- *Read the book chapter once. After that, use it as a reference for things you don't understand from the notes, lecture, and homework problems.*
- *Do homework. You may not be asked to turn it in but you might be able to count on seeing problems from it appearing on tests.*
- *Study with friends. You can help each other and the helper learns easily as much in explaining it to the helpee. Any professor can tell you that they never learned the material as well as when they taught it. You will also keep going and focussed in a group— misery loves company. And you can write test questions for each other. It helps you see what you do and don't know. And you can often psych out what I will ask you.*

## Physics
Many students avoid physics like the plague. Pre-medical students spend some time wondering why they even have to learn about circuits and harmonic motion when they will be working with

patients and illness. You must realize that physics underlies almost every other science. Understanding physics will allow you to appreciate biological and chemical properties in nature. Keep that in mind when you are stuck in a physics lab trying to work with your oscilloscope.

## Biology

Most students who are pursuing medicine believe that biology is all medicine is about, but just because you are good in biology does not mean that you will make a good doctor. Biology requires the ability to retain facts and apply them in foreign situations.

Many students incorrectly shrug off biology as a memorization course. They will be surprised when the MCAT doesn't ask them to define photosynthesis or list the components of deoxyribose nucleic acid. Memorization will only get you so far in the race to medical school; proper understanding will get you to the finish line.

## Memory devices

Sometimes you are asked to recall a list of facts. What do you do? Many students have their own way of storing information. People are all wired differently in the brain. Some devices work better for some than others. It is your task to find out what works for you and to stick to it.

### Mnemonics

A very popular device is the traditional mnemonic. It is a word or string that is intended to be easier to remember than what it stands for. A mnemonic can be a formula, rhyme, or acronym. For example, in hydrogen bonding, there are usually three atoms associated with it. The mnemonic "FON" is used to remember that they are Fluorine, Oxygen, and Nitrogen. In chemistry, you might have heard of "OIL RIG" to remember that "Oxidation Is the Loss of electrons," while "Reductions Is the Gain of electrons." There are several of these devices.

If there isn't one for the particular list of facts you are memorizing, make up your own. Relate it to your best friend, favorite sport, etc. However, do not let mnemonic devices replace learning the concepts behind the list of facts that you are memorizing. If memorizing the pathway of digestion, don't forget to learn the structure and function of each organ as well.

## Application

Another way to learn new concepts is to apply them to everyday life. You may think this is going overboard, but you will be surprised at how useful it really is. For example, suppose you just learned about projectile motion in physics. The next time you throw a football, remember that the horizontal component of velocity is constant and that gravity only affects the vertical component. Warning: pointing this out to football buddies may result in getting your butt kicked!

It might not seem like a big deal, but relating supposedly abstract concepts to real-life situations helps you appreciate and understand them. Here's what a neurologist told us:

> In graduate school, I was interested in doing things that would improve my mind's ability to educate itself. The mind is simply a physiological entity. Learning about health (i.e., exercise, diet) taught me a lot of physiology and anatomy at the molecular and cellular levels, especially.
>
> D.A. Personett

## Taking notes

Taking good notes is vital to academic success. Save whatever notes you have for later reference, especially for the MCAT. The MCAT tests several academic subjects and old notes will be a vital resource. This should also be a motivating factor to keep those notes orderly and neat. Some students rewrite notes because it allows them to reinforce what they have learned in lecture.

Notes also provide insight into possible test questions of many professors. If a professor writes something on a board, or mentions it several times in lecture, you should take *note* of it. It just might appear on a test. You may also consider asking upperclassmen for their notes and old tests to prepare for exams. It is likely that professors ask similar questions from year to year and studying the right material will guarantee success.

## Writing essays and papers

Writing essays can sometimes be a painstaking task. Many science-oriented students have a difficult time with their non-objective classes. However, it is vital that you can clearly organize your thoughts on paper. The MCAT has a writing section that specifically tests this ability. If you have trouble writing essays, take writing seminars that are offered in your school.

A good exercise to develop your creative writing skills is to pick a random topic and write as much as you can about it. Then organize it into an essay and ask an English professor to critique it.

## Recovering from failure

Failure is something that we all must face at some point in our lives. Contrary to popular belief, failure is not always a negative thing, and instead it tells you that you are doing something wrong so that you can fix it. It develops character and reveals inner strength, and those individuals who suck it up, remedy the problem, and continue to try their hardest are the ones that are usually successful.

A bad grade on one test in college will not force you to drop out of a program. You must keep things in perspective and retain some form of optimism. The greatest champions have endured defeat on their road to victory.

### Seeking help

Knowing and admitting that you need help in a certain area is a necessary character trait for any pre-med hoping to keep his sanity. In order to best help yourself, make sure that you reach out at the very first signs of trouble—before facing irreversible failure. Waiting until the last minute to seek help is the worst possible thing you can do for yourself because you will inevitably fall behind in the course, achieve low test scores, and prevent yourself from effectively learning the material. Professors and advisors are there to provide you with academic support and moral guidance, so take advantage of these available resources.

## Mastering the "Shi"

Despite all this advice, some teachers seem like they are on a mission to make their classes very taxing. How do you handle these situations? That is where your mindset must step it up and take you that extra mile. You must go into a test, presentation, and or classroom environment with the confidence that you can tackle whatever they throw at you.

This state of mind has various names associated with it from "Chi" to "Mojo." We like to call it "Shi." When you know it's about to hit the fan, you have to be ready and master the "Shi."

- Never study things you already know. Concentrate on novel information.
- Achieve a balance between work and play. Avoid extremes of each.
- Feel confident that you can overcome any obstacle in the face of adversity.

- When you succeed, don't let it go to your head. When you fail, understand why you did so and how to move on from that point.
- Get to know your professor and how he thinks, questions, and teaches. Knowing what to expect is half the battle.
- Know yourself and what you are capable of doing. Procrastinators enjoy working under pressure and do their best work under those conditions. Organizers like to plan out their study schedules and stick to them.
- Most importantly, never give up. By giving up you admit to defeat and have truly lost.

Many pre-medical students are anal retentive. They spend hours memorizing trivial facts and put all their efforts to achieving the perfect test score. You rarely see them outside the library or dorm room before a test.

Intense work and no play does not even guarantee success. Who wants to live like that? They are usually pompous, competitive, and unfriendly. They obviously have not mastered the "Shi." You must realize that good doctors are compassionate, understanding, and able to handle all sorts of situations. Try not to fall into this negative pre-medical mindset. Find the "Shi" within you.

# CHAPTER 15

## College Activities and Social Life

*"It's not your blue blood, your pedigree or your college degree.
It's what you do with your life that counts."*
—Millard Fuller

*"Ask me about microwaving cats for fun and profit."*
—Bumper Sticker

Your studies will keep you busy, but nobody can study and do homework all day and all night, and nor should they. No matter what your schedule is like, you will still have time for a social life and to be active on campus. One student told us, "I feel like I have enough time to get involved, except of course, around finals period."

## Extra-curricular

Many programmers become lazy when it comes to activities unrelated to their specific courses because they have a near-guarantee of acceptance to medical school and feel that they have already "paid their dues" in high school.

Time becomes your enemy in college and time management is crucial for programmers because they are accelerated by 1-2 years. This means they'll have less time to date, party, and just plain vegetate.

Some worthwhile activities in college include various clubs, honors societies, sports, political positions, service, journalism, performing arts, etc. If your school doesn't have the specific club that you are looking for, take the initiative to establish it and leave your legacy.

While it is important to be involved on campus, don't spread yourself *too* thin. Also make sure that you are always above your requirements because your primary objective is to get an education and prepare yourself for medical school.

**Clubs and teams**
A good way to meet people is by joining clubs and teams such as sports, theatre and music, newspaper, television, radio, etc. This college sophomore has found an activity that has allowed him to make a lot of great friends:

> *Being a member of an acapella group is one of the best things that has ever happened to me. Singing is one of my favorite things in the world to do. And to do it in front of an audience is just a high that I can't get anywhere else. It's indescribable. Also, you get so very close to the other members of the group. We aren't just a bunch of people that love to sing together, we are a family.*
>
> *You have a special connection with the other members of the group. It's funny what you talk about if you're stuck in a car with someone for 10 plus hours. Also, you are in the same boat with the other members in terms of academics. We attend Johns Hopkins University, a very competitive school, and it's tough to keep your head above water especially if you have a thing like an acapella group that takes a lot of your precious time.*
>
> *I think that all us members have to find a way to juggle our academic schedules with the group. There are a handful of members in my group that are pre-med. They also MUST keep everything together. It's these connections that make the friendship within the group special. These connections are what make us a family.*
>
> *Mark Ferarris*

## Volunteering

There are many reasons that volunteering can be a meaningful experience. You will meet people, feel good about yourself, and build your résumé—not to mention that you will get to help people, something that you should enjoy if you are going to become a doctor. You may not have had significant volunteering experiences in the past. The following Swarthmore College student recommends opening your mind to trying new things:

> A lot of new college students, especially those who enter BA/ MD programs, think they have it all figured out—they know who they are, what they are going to be, and what they are interested in. The undergraduate years allow an opportunity to take a step back and challenge these understandings.
>
> Doing something completely new, something that had never even entered into consideration, is an excellent way for college students to test their conceptions of themselves. For me, it was becoming a volunteer firefighter. Certainly, firefighting had never entered my mind as even a remotely possible college extracurricular activity.
>
> I signed up for the fire department on a whim of sorts. The thing that is probably the most distinctive about the fire department is that, unlike so many of my other college activities, it is absolutely the real deal. With many of the other things I do at Swarthmore, I get the feeling that we are playing pretend. We go through the motions that people do in the real world, but it is just practicing. There is simply no room for going through the motions in the fire department.
>
> This attitude is indoctrinated in new firefighters via the extensive training we are required to go through. For me, the realization of how seriously I had to treat it came at the end of my introductory firefighting course. It was our final burn day, we had learned the essentials, and it was time to put them to the

*test by simulating different kinds of structure fires in the aptly named "burn building."*

*Unfortunately, one student treated the class lightly and got hurt because of it. I don't think anyone who was part of that fire school class will ever forget the lesson of that day. The fire department has allowed me the opportunity to be a part of something both excellent and genuine.*

*Will Ortman*

## Research

Some students love research and find a way to incorporate it into their college years. One motivating factor is that it will benefit you on your overall résumé for application to residency programs later down the road. Doing college-level research places you in a great position to publish a paper, discover a medical breakthrough, and to leave your mark in research. Finally, research develops great critical thinking skills and other traits beneficial to a physician.

It is easier to obtain a research position in college than in high school because you can team up with your professor on his or her work. This close personal relationship will also be perfect for obtaining letters of recommendation. Colleges are known for being institutions of discovery, and doing research may also benefit you by affording you credits.

## Sports

Participating on a sporting team can be a very worthwhile activity, as well. Whether or not you join a team, you should at least consider exercising. A regular workout program is key to maintaining a healthy and happy lifestyle. University of Pennsylvania sophomore Frank Minetti recommends working out and staying in shape for several reasons:

*When the semester progresses and the workload gets rougher, most pre-med students tend not to leave their rooms because they feel that they should be concentrating on schoolwork. What they don't realize is that most of the time they spend "studying" is useless, because they are always getting up and talking to friends, chatting on the Internet, etc.*

*A regular workout program allows one to structure his or her time better and forces one to actually study during "study time." Besides, after extended studying, the mind begins to get bogged down. Working out is a perfect break to relieve stress, and get back and focus on studying.*

*When you workout regularly, your physical appearance begins to improve. With improved looks comes a natural increase in self-confidence, which leads to a better social life. Of course, it is important to remember that random weightlifting does absolutely no good. The real key to improvement is to create a schedule and stick with it.*

## Greek life

If you are looking to make many life-long friends and have some great memories before you leave college, you may consider joining a fraternity or sorority.

Some schools have a strong Greek life, with as many as fifty fraternities and sororities on campus. Sometimes more than 50% of the student body participates, and it can dominate the social landscape.

At some schools pledging can be extremely rough. If this is the case, you can just forget about it! Not only can pledging sometimes be physically dangerous but it can monopolize all your time and deprive you of sleep. These two obstacles can be enough to hurt your GPA beyond repair. Ask the older students how pledging is at a typical house. Generally sororities are not as bad as fraternities, but there are always exceptions.

Also think about what kind of environment you will be in if you decide to live in the fraternity or sorority. You don't want to be somewhere that you know will always have distractions. On the other hand, a little self-motivation is all you need to walk to the library to get your work done. If you have good time management, you should be able to pull everything off.

Some fraternities may be nice places to hang out, but you wouldn't want to live there. Most likely, if your school has a big Greek life, your friends will pledge and even if you don't, you'll still have social ties. The majority of programmers will not pledge because of their dedication to academics and their short time in college.

Even if you have no intention of pledging, you can still rush. Usually fraternity rush is over a period of a few months where you hang out with the brothers and meet a lot of people. Sorority rush can consist of a week long formal rush period. Successful rush will result in a bid, which is an invitation to join. Either way, there is no commitment to pledge.

> *When I started school at Lehigh, I had no intention of rushing or pledging at all. That is until, everyone on my hall started hanging out at fraternities every night. I got on some lists and was invited to events, but I didn't really like any houses in particular. Finally, I journeyed up to the top of the hill to Sigma Alpha Mu (Sammy), and I had an awesome night. I really liked the guys there and I began to hang out there more often. Eventually I received a bid, and I decided to pledge.*
>
> *Pledging Sammy was one of the best decisions that I've ever made, besides attending an accelerated medical program in the first place. I've made so many friends and had so much fun, that I don't feel like I've missed out by only going to college for two years. I feel like traditional pre-meds have to work so hard, that they end up having less fun in their four years than I've had in my two.*
>
> *Jason Yanofski*

## Partying

Whether you get involved in Greek life or not, no matter where you go to school, you will have at least some opportunity to party, drink, and do drugs. Obviously substance abuse and accelerated medical programs don't mix. Experimentation is usually harmless, but not always, because all people have different tolerances, and some people have very addictive personalities.

You really need to be careful with everything you do, as a programmer. Your guarantee is conditional, and trouble that you get yourself into will show immaturity and be grounds for dismissal. So, if you are going to drink, do so responsibly. This means that you should be in a safe environment with friends, and always use designated drivers.

One of the most important things that you will need to learn if you want to get by in college is self-control. Every night there will be people on your hall going out to party or just hanging out, and it can be tempting to do the same. If you party every night, however, your grades will drop severely. What you need to keep in mind is that it's different people that are going out each night, and when people are studying, they are in their rooms or the library, and so you don't see that.

## Peer interactions

Being a programmer entails certain responsibilities and certain ways of conduct. Do not act overconfident or as if you're better than others in your university, especially those within your own program. In fact, you should try and build positive and supportive relationships with your fellow programmers. After all, you will be spending many years with them in the future. You may have heard stories of traditional pre-med students being cutthroat and doing whatever it takes to eliminate the competition.

In an accelerated med-program, there is no need for this Darwinian philosophy. You and your fellow programmers will be going to the same medical school. Since you are all highly motivated and intelligent students, you should work *with* each other and not *against* each other. You can study together, exchange notes, and even do research together. You will be surprised at the achievements that can be made when great minds get together – like this book!

Of course, not everyone in college will be in the program. The vast majority will not even be aware of the existence of the program without knowing someone in it. Most college students are undecided of their major and may be apprehensive about their future. Having a programmer walk up to them and elucidate the next 6-7 years of their life perfectly laid out will be quite disheartening for them. Keep this in mind during interactions with friends and acquaintances. This warning should be amplified for your friends who are pre-med but not in the program.

Not everyone is supportive of the program. Jealousy and other negative emotions may be directed at you simply because you have an opportunity that others don't have. Programmers are very mature, are highly motivated, and they become successful doctors. This is not to say that traditional pre-med students don't posses these qualities, and they aren't as qualified to become doctors.

Be compassionate and don't flaunt your fortunate position. Remember that each year many highly qualified students are rejected both from medical degree programs and traditional medical school simply because the system cannot absorb them.

## Traveling

Aside from being a new experience, for some students, college can be a whole new world all together. This is especially true for students who travel great distances to receive their education. After making the tough decision to leave home, the last thing they want to face is social and cultural hardships of a new environment and the annoyances of planes, buses, trains, etc.

Jonathan Popkin-Paine told us:

> *When I went to school in Pennsylvania after living in Texas my whole life, I experienced quite a culture shock. If you can go someplace you've never been, where you don't know anyone, it will definitely become a character building experience. My family can afford to fly me back and forth even on small holidays, so the decision was a good one. You will find that you'll always be able to develop support groups with others in your situation.*

## Commuting

If you are strapped financially and lucky enough to attend a program close to home, you may be able to save money by commuting. However, other than the difficulty of commuting itself, another problem is the fact that you are not always accessible or on campus. People that live on campus will not understand that for you to meet at nine on a weeknight is just not possible. Eventually, you will learn how to work around such problems.

But there are perks to commuting, too. You still have the luxury of having your parents around. When you get home from a long day of school, you can look forward to having dinner on the table, and maybe your clothes will be washed. Not that you can't take care of yourself, but you'll have certain benefits that the average college student does not have.

If you live at home, your relationship with your parents will have to change. They will have to treat you like an adult. They know just how hard it is for you to commute to school, and they should respect you for sticking to your decision. Here is how one college sophomore has dealt with her decision to commute:

> *When I was accepted at NYU under the early decision plan, I knew that I was going and nothing was going to stop me. I also knew that I would not be living on campus. I had*

*discussed it with my parents and the decision was final: if I wanted to go there that I was going to have to commute. But, I have to say; I never really grasped just how difficult it would be. I realized that quite a few things would restrict me, and that of course I would not have the "typical college experience." But I was willing to take the good with the bad.*

*The first week of commuting was probably the most difficult for me. The campus is approximately 45 minutes from my house. And my commute is not an easy one. I have to first drive to the train station, take one train for about a half hour, then jump onto another train for 12 minutes, and then walk 5 blocks.*

*Commuting was nothing like I had ever done before. And I didn't know how I was going to make it through the four years. I remember thinking that maybe I had made a horrible mistake. But, as time went on, I got into a routine.*

*I truly believe that where there is a will there is a way. So far I've been commuting for almost 2 years, and I can truly say that though it's not the "typical college experience" it is definitely an experience. One that I wouldn't change for anything, not even a dorm room!*

*Maria Maragos*

# CHAPTER 16

## The MCAT

*"In the fields of observation chance
favors only the prepared mind."*
—Louis Pasteur

*"Even if you are on the right track, you'll
get run over if you just sit there."*
—Will Rogers

## Overview

Traditional students, knowing that they will eventually have to face the Medical College Admissions Test (MCAT), are forced to pay extra attention in class. They need to study for months to remember all the physics, chemistry, and biology that they've learned over the last few years. Most importantly, they need to perform under pressure and prove themselves.

### Will I have to take the MCAT?

Depending on the program, there are three possibilities. In the first possibility, you may not have to ever take the MCAT. Lucky, lucky you. The MCAT is a very long, very annoying test. It makes the SAT look like a joke. The whole experience is about eight hours long, with actual testing lasting six and one-half hours. The difference is in the hour lunch break and ten-minute breaks in between sections.

The second possibility is that you have to take the MCAT as a mere formality but it will not count toward your acceptance to medical school. The third possibility is that you will have to take the MCAT and achieve certain scores on each section in order to gain admission.

## Pass/fail mentality

If you are taking the test early, it is likely that you have not taken the necessary courses for proper preparation—sounds a little scary? However, remember that you usually have a set score on each section you are shooting for. Because of this set score, many accelerated students tackle the test with a pass/fail mentality.

If they get the required scores, they've "passed," and that's good enough to move on. If they don't, they have "failed" and must try again if they have that chance. Whatever the case may be, try to do your best given the circumstances.

## When to take it

You may have a limit on how many times you can take the MCAT until you pass, usually three times. Even if this is the case, you will still need to pass before you go on to medical school, and the test is only given twice a year, in April and August.

*Traditional students* usually take it once and then only retake it if they feel that they can significantly improve their scores. Low past scores or decreasing scores are not preferred by admissions.

For the most part, *programmers* aren't really trying to impress anybody. So taking the MCAT early for experience might not be a bad idea. However, a practice test may be more efficient for that purpose and would definitely be cheaper.

Any time you go to take the MCAT, you should take it seriously because if you pass, you will be very glad that you did. This is not the kind of test that you want to take more times than you need to. You will have to wait at least several months and retain all the previously learned information.

It will be virtually impossible to pass a requirement on a particular section without any knowledge about one or more of the topics (passing biological section without ever having organic chemistry, for example). Our advice is that as soon as you have taken every class that you need, it is a good time to review and practice for a few weeks, and take the MCAT for the first time. Try to plan it for when you'll have time to study hardcore for at least two or three weeks prior to the test. This is a good idea even if you are taking difficult courses all year round.

If your program is a six-year program, then it may be difficult to complete all necessary courses before taking the MCAT, especially if you came in without any credit or if you've had to retake any courses. This is something that you will need to think about if you have the choice between six or seven years in your program. Find out if you can plan on a six-year route, but then still have that extra year as a back up, in case you don't pass your test.

## Preparation

You will need to study for the MCAT. Just like any college exam, you will have to review the materials because a lot is covered, and just like any standardized exam, you have to be familiar with the format and timing to take the test efficiently. Just because you did well in all your basic sciences doesn't mean that you will do well on the MCAT. If you underestimate this test, you are likely to regret it.

It is important to review your two semesters each of biology, chemistry, physics, and organic chemistry. Since you are in the program, you had most of your courses crammed into your last few semesters. You may actually have an easier time than a traditional student, who wouldn't have had these courses for two or more years. However be cautious: if you placed out of some of your science courses, make sure you still have a grasp on all the concepts covered in those courses.

It will help to have a strong social science and humanities background when taking the verbal reasoning section. The passages are usually from fields such as economics, psychology, art, history, law, and philosophy. It may not to be worth taking any particular class just for this verbal section, but an overall strong background may make a big difference in your understanding of specific passages. Keep in mind that no actual previous background knowledge is required to answer any of the questions.

There are many ways to go about studying for the MCAT. You could take a course, either one offered by your school or a commercial one. These courses are a comprehensive review of all your sciences and offer a lot of extra resources (practice tests, etc). These courses can cost one thousand dollars or more and may not be necessary for self-motivated students. At the very minimum, you should buy a book that will help you review your sciences, give you test taking advice, and offer practice tests.

In the month before the test, you should take at least two full-length practice tests a week. This will build up your stamina and familiarize you with the types of questions asked on the actual exam. If you are the type of person who will procrastinate your studying and not take practice tests on your own, taking a course may be in your best interest.

### What skills does the MCAT test?
The MCAT tests **thinking skills, facts, and concepts.** In a way, it is also somewhat of an endurance test. It is difficult for someone who has not experienced a six hour exam to be able to concentrate and reason things out for that period of time—let alone just sit in the same chair! The fact that biology, the subject most pre-meds are most familiar with, is always the last section probably isn't a coincidence.

# MCAT format

The MCAT is divided into the sections: physical sciences, biological sciences, verbal reasoning, and the writing sample. The verbal (85 minutes) and science (100 minutes) sections are graded on a scale from 1 to 15, 15 being the highest score. The writing sample (60 minutes) is oddly graded from J to T, T being the highest score. You will have short breaks between sections and a lunch break in the middle. Unlike the SAT, there is no penalty for guessing on the multiple-choice questions, so don't leave anything blank.

## Physical sciences
The physical sciences section is about half physics and half chemistry in content. You will need to know how to work with a lot of formulas. Often the formulas are not complex but the given applications are. You will to be able to understand what you need to do to answer what you are being asked. You will also have to be able to use concepts together that you have not used together before.

## Biological sciences
The biological sciences section is part biology questions and is part organic chemistry questions, though significantly more biology. Knowledge of specific facts is important for biology, and many passages require you to be familiar with how experiments are set up. Organic chemistry requires knowledge of first semester concepts and some more obscure ones.

## Verbal reasoning
The verbal reasoning section requires you to be able to quickly read about a variety of mature topics, understand the basic idea of what you are reading, and reapply the information in critical thinking questions. The section is titled appropriately because you *do* need to use reason and inference in order to determine which is the best answer.

While you can improve your science section scores by reviewing the material, the verbal section is the most difficult to improve upon and to do so, you must practice, practice, practice! Without prior experience with the MCAT, it may seem like a shock to be hit with an art or economics passage early on, so be prepared.

### Writing section

Medical schools do not usually stress the writing section, and so it carries less importance. You will get two half-hour essays, in which you will need to examine a broad or ambiguous statement. A good score will come from answering the questions fully and precisely, as well as writing creatively, at a sophisticated level, and with few grammatical errors.

# Q&A

### If I'm a good test taker, will I be able to perform well on the MCAT?

The MCAT is very different than the SAT in terms of length, content, and difficulty, but the same basic skills are necessary. The MCAT contains a verbal section that is much harder than the one on the SAT, and the science sections are math intensive. While test-taking skills are important, without the proper preparation, you will not be able to perform up to your maximum potential.

### Will having experience of upper level science courses help in the physical and biological sections?

Upper level courses will not be of assistance unless, due to previously learned material, you happen to understand beforehand what a passage is trying to explain as a "new" concept, or if taking the course makes lower level science seem easy and basic in comparison.

### I need to get the national average score of 9's in the three sections. How many questions does that mean that I'll have to get right?

The number of questions that you'll need to answer correctly varies between the three sections, which are always scaled individually. The verbal reasoning section fluctuates the most. You will need to get around 80% of the questions right to get a nine, though if you find your passages particularly easy, this means that you probably can't afford to get more than just a few wrong.

The science sections are more constant. Nines in the physical and biological sciences will be given for answering about 50% and 60% of the questions right, respectively. These percentages are good to know, because otherwise you may be mislead into thinking that you performed better on your verbal than your sciences, but actually scored much higher in the sciences, due to the scale.

**Why should I try to get higher than my required score?**
- Scholarships
- Aiming higher gives you a better chance at passing comfortably
- Chance to apply out of the program to other medical schools (See Chapter 17)

At the Rice University program the MCAT is not required. However, taking the MCAT is recommended if one is interested in application to the medical school's MD/PhD or MD/MBA programs. (See Chapter 19)

# UNIT V

## Success!

# CHAPTER 17

## Leaving the Program

*"The only real mistake is the one from
which we learn nothing."*
—John Powell

*"A man is not finished when he's defeated;
he's finished when he quits."*
—Richard Nixon

You survived your two or three undergraduate years and you are still in the program. It's time to move on. The first part of this chapter will explain all the things that you need to do to prepare yourself to leave. The rest of the chapter will explain other options that you may want to keep in mind and how to handle being released.

## Med. Application

You will most likely need to fill out a standard application form for the medical school. This will include a personal statement and recommendations. You will have forms specific to program students *and* some that are universal to all applicants. Here is an example of an effective personal statement:

> *When I was a kid, I would grab my mother's red towel,*
> *wrap it around my neck, climb the couch, and attempt to defy*

*gravity. Free fall was quickly discovered in my first experiment. A few weeks later, I found some string and attempted to construct a web as Spiderman. I even went to the library and checked out Charlotte's Web thinking that it was a secret document that would show me how to make a web. I climbed a cabinet to reach the sewing kit on the top shelf. The string was eventually obtained along with eight stitches from the fall.*

*After my wounds healed, super-powers were no longer pursued. I would fight crime as Batman. Talcum powder, flashlight, cardboard, and bicycle were gathered. The talcum powder worsened my childhood asthma, and my neighbors wondered why a little boy rode his bicycle with cardboard flaps and flashlight. The flashlight was for the bat signal of course. Unfortunately, batteries were overlooked. I can't remember what the flaps were for. Finally, I had training wheels that prevented me from engaging in high-speed pursuits.*

*Many people may look at these childhood stories and enjoy the genuine humor of it all. However, being on the verge of entering medical school, I realize that my childhood and whole life experience to date have been far deeper. When I fell off the couch, I should have known that falling was natural and inevitable. That might have prevented me from climbing the cabinet and hurting myself. I had to learn the life lesson "hard way." Thus, ever since then, I have questioned and spoken to several individuals for the sake of knowledge in important aspects of my life.*

*Before even applying to college, I took the extra effort in considering many other professions only to realize that medicine was right for me. When I read Charlotte's Web, I encountered death for the first time. The concept was foreign to me. However, the seed of the reality of life and death was planted. I have learned the important role that doctors play in preserving life. No other profession can be as rewarding for me. As a child, I thought the way to save lives was to have super-powers, hi-tech gadgets, and a Batmobile. I now realize that to save lives, all I need are knowledge and the ability to make wise decisions.*

*In my years at Lehigh, I have continued to foster my pursuit of knowledge and the ability to make wise decisions. I have taken courses that will develop my character as a complete person. Philosophy, bioethics, law, and economics are a few. Just because you are a doctor does not mean that you need only know about anatomy and biology. Leonardo da Vinci is the epitome of what I value as the complete individual. He was an artist, engineer, scientist, sculptor, and much more. Though I can only attempt to be as accomplished, I apply such a renaissance philosophy in my academic life. Many of my peers don't believe that I am pursuing medicine when they see my schedule of classes from Y2K to Kantian Ethics. Leadership and service are also important in my life. These activities enable me to apply my knowledge in a positive setting. I am the president of my residential village, the member of a national service fraternity, tutor, and member of the Global Union. I have made friendships that will last a lifetime and developed relationships with others that I could never have imagined. My experience at Lehigh is priceless. I cannot begin to describe the wonderful adventures, humorous mishaps, and genuine love I have felt in college. I can only hope others have been able to see, hear, and feel what I have. In the end, I may not be able to wear a cape. However, a lab coat and scrubs are fine with me!*

*Ashish Raju*

## When do I need to let the medical school know?

Always keep in touch with your advisor about time issues. At some point, she should call you in for a meeting to discuss the application process. You should start thinking about this in November or December. You will not have to go by the application deadlines of traditional applicants.

**I have a guaranteed spot, so why do I need to go through more application forms?**

As a programmer, the medical school application is a formality. Every student, whether they are coming from a program or not, will have to fill out an AMCAS application if their medical school is AAMC affiliated. This information is required for statistical/demographical purposes in order to build a database of information about each of the students that make up medical schools' 16,000 seats.

**Should I be worrying?**

As long as you have met your academic requirements and go through the paperwork competently, you should not have anything to worry about. The medical school will do a final evaluation and meet with your advisor to discuss your application. The scrutiny with which you are examined before matriculation varies from school to school.

This is not to say that you shouldn't take your application seriously. It is in your best interest to write a good personal statement and attempt to get positive recommendations. Some medical schools will deny acceptance to students for maturity reasons even if they have met all other program requirements. Discuss this with your advisor if you have concerns. She will be able to let you know if students have been denied admission in the past.

**What if I haven't received passing MCAT scores yet?**

If you have not yet received a passing MCAT score, you should be able to send out the application and take the test that April or August.

**Visiting the medical school**

This should be a very exciting time for you. You should take a trip to the medical school some day and explore the town, if it isn't on the university campus. You can start looking at places to live if the school doesn't provide dormitories.

Remember, you are already ahead of the game. Most people that you will be with in medical school next year don't even know that they will be there yet. You already do know, and hopefully, you also have a group of friends that are coming with you.

## Applying out

Not everyone who starts his or her college career in an accelerated medical program ends it that way. They may chose to resign for a number of reasons, or they may be kicked out, also for a number of different reasons. The rest of this chapter looks at both sides of leaving the program and how to handle it.

Normally, if you want to apply to a medical school other than the one that your program is affiliated with, you will be released and lose your conditional acceptance. In some cases, though risky, it is possible that doing so may be the best decision for you in the long run. This section, "Applying out," was written by ex-accelerated (decelerated? deprogrammed?) student Anil Trindade. He gives his advice on leaving the program to apply to other medical schools.

**Why would someone want to leave the program?**
Somewhere in the stage of the medical program track, there are some reasons that a student may consider leaving the confines of the medical program and, instead, applying to medical schools as a traditional applicant.

While medical programs do provide for a more relaxing undergraduate experience, one negative aspect is that most programs detract from the college years – literally. In fact, within the medical community, accelerated programs are often despised, and it is said that they foster physicians who lack the maturity that only time can bring.

Oftentimes, students in their final semesters of the undergraduate years in the program come to this realization. Or rather, it's the combination of having to leave an environment that's safe, yet exciting and fun, and enter the demanding realm of medical school at an age that's premature, (the average age of first year medical students is 25), that prevents students from wanting to continue with the program.

There are several reasons why a student may pursue this course of action. While programs offer the assurance of a seat in medical school, sometimes it is to schools that fall in the third or fourth tiers of national rankings.

## Is the quality of the medical school important?

Most program students who decide to drop the program do so in pursuit of a seat to a more esteemed institution. This scenario necessitates the question, "Does it matter which medical school I go to?" Unfortunately, the answer isn't as clear as one would hope for. It largely depends on the ambitions and goals that one has for their medical career – things that are not certain even to older students.

For those who are content with a private practice in general medicine or pediatrics, most medical schools are sufficient for obtaining a good education and residency program and for eventually operating a successful practice.

The quality of school is more pertinent when specialty fields, research, and/or a career in academic medicine are desired. Although the acceptances to top residency programs are based largely in performance on the USMLE board examinations, a student coming from a very respected school having performed satisfactorily clearly has an advantage over a person from a less renowned school.

It is not to say that a student coming from a lower ranked medical school is precluded from top residency positions. Instead, such a candidate will have to work harder to capture a favored residency.

For those interested in academic medicine or research, MD/PhD programs may be suitable. Such a program allows a student to earn both degrees in seven or eight years. In addition to career advantages, schools generally offer a tuition waive as well as a stipend of about $12,000 per year.

### Financial

Another possible reason for wanting to leave a medical program, especially an accelerated one, is financial. What many medical schools fail to explain to prospective program students is that they are often ineligible for merit-based scholarships, at least during the first year. Although the reasons vary, a primary one is that program students generally do not receive their undergraduate degrees until the completion of the first or second year of medical school, therefore neglecting them to a status inferior to the traditional degree-bearing applicant. This lack of eligibility for merit-based awards can often mean the difference of thousands of dollars.

### Should *I* drop?

When considering whether or not to drop an accelerated medical program, several issues must be weighed out. Foremost, are your grades and MCAT scores competitive? Since many program students neglect participating in community service and medically related and leadership activities in college because they don't have to, it should be determined whether your résumé is up to par.

When applying to medical school, there is one question that you should always ask yourself – How unique am I? If you can answer this question by citing concrete examples, then you're already one step ahead of the game.

Finally, be sure that you have developed good relations with several faculty and staff members, for it is important to have excellent letters of recommendation.

### Are you ready to leave college?

A student may not feel ready to leave college at an age of 19 or 20. Attending college for two or three years often leaves a student yearning for more, especially one who is involved in Greek life, clubs, sports, research, or other such commitments that span the length of the college career. It is usually in the junior and senior year of college that leadership roles or other such rewards are granted.

Not having these experiences may often leave a student feeling deprived.

### Are you ready to go to medical school?

For those students who feel unprepared to leave college, a natural corollary would be the dread of beginning medical school at an undeveloped stage. Such a dread is valid. Academically, program students may not be ready to undertake the demands of medical school courses, especially when the depth of university undergraduate classes barely extended beyond introductory topics.

In such instances, program students may be less knowledgeable, which starts them off towards the bottom of the class. Consequent psychological reactions are then likely to result, especially for those students who are used to being at the top.

Program students often suffer socially as well. Not only have they departed from their college friends, but making new ones in an environment that's usually not socially conducive, and that's filled with peers who are three or four years older is extremely difficult.

Students who are under 21 may feel especially isolated, for it is common practice to "hit the bars" after exams, a practice that they cannot legally participate in. Additionally, medical school is often the forum where one meets his or her spouse, which could prove difficult to do when the age barrier is extensive.

### How do I drop out?

Although this is a seemingly simplistic question, it is important to drop the program in a manner that maintains good relations with your program advisor, for it is usually he or she that advises traditional applicants as well. The best way is to discuss your reasoning informally with your advisor. A polite formal letter to your advisor and medical school should then follow. The letter should have tones of gratefulness for awarding a seat for you. At the same time, be strong and firm, because that's how you should feel about your decision.

**Other reasons to leave**

Besides looking at better medical schools, you may decide that medical school is not for you at all. It's not too late to change your mind. Consider the time you spent during your past college years as a learning experience, but now you need to start looking in other directions. It is not extremely uncommon for pre-med majors to end up in business, law, research, engineering, or even other health professions.

## Being kicked out

The accelerated medical program is a rigorous route, and it is not for everybody. Did you party too much and let your GPA take a nosedive? Were your MCAT scores just not where they needed to be? For the most part, medical schools will be extremely strict with their original requirements. Just as you need a specific SAT score just to apply, if your final grade point average is too low, even if by only .01, you're probably going to have a problem.

If you are in a gray area, you should talk to your advisor. You need to find out where you stand and what you can do about it. For example, if your GPA isn't cutting it, are you allowed to stay an extra year or summer session to improve it, or do you lose your spot automatically?

**Maturity clause**

In your program contract, there will generally be a clause about maturity or some loophole that allows the medical school not to take you if you've gotten involved with any sort of trouble. Your guarantee is only conditional, and though the medical school isn't looking for ways to get rid of you, it may not ignore them either. If you have gotten into trouble that resulted in probation, suspension, etc., you will want to write a letter explaining the situation and include it with your application.

Usually, the opinion of your advisor will play a big role in this case. They act as a liaison between you and the school, and they may be asked if they feel that you are ready to matriculate into medical school. Hopefully they will stand behind you with full support.

If you find out that for some reason the medical school has decided not to accept you, find out why—if you don't already know. If you don't feel that the reason is fair, you may want to try to petition it, or get a hearing in front of admissions. After all, you did have a contract, and you do deserve an explanation. This is your whole life we are talking about here!

## Released from the program

In the end, if you are released, don't give up on your dreams. It doesn't necessarily mean that you won't be going to medical school in the future. It just means that it will take more time, and you will need to work a little harder. Sure, it stinks, but "you gotta do whatcha gotta do." Hopefully, you haven't already signed a lease for any apartments. For more information about failure, see Chapter 10.

> *Ever since I've been involved in the accelerated program, it seems as if I've been given obstacles to overcome. My biggest obstacle came when I was preparing to start my last semester after my first relaxing break from school.*
>
> *I was confused as to why I received an "F" on my report card, which arrived on December 31, 1999. I thought the world was ending! The apocalypse was upon us! It was for a biology course in which I had expected to receive an "A." I was waiting for that report card so that I could fill out my final application to matriculate into medical school, but I had to put that on hold, being that I wasn't allowed to receive any grade lower than a "C." I eventually found out that I had been accused of plagiarism on my final presentation project.*
>
> *After all the work I had done, I was not prepared to give up without a fight. I found out that there was a judicial department, set up to deal with issues like this. My case was strong and*

*in the end, the panel decided in my favor. I did not cheat and received my deserved "A." Justice was served. The lesson learned: I was very lucky to be in an accelerated medical program, and I will be much more careful in the future so as not to put my entire career on the line.*

Dick Atkinson

## Summary

Here are the most likely reasons that someone would leave an accelerated medical program before they've finished it:

- Upon entering a specialized program, they realize that medicine isn't their calling. They may like computer science, law, or some other field after being exposed to it in college.
- After taking several classes and doing extremely well on the MCAT, certain students may want to drop the program and apply to more prestigious medical schools. They don't like the fact that they are locked into one specific program.
- Location, family, or friends may sway individuals away from a particular medical school.
- The student may not have met the academic requirements necessary to stay in the program and are forced to leave.
- Academic misconduct or other improper behavior will also release one from a program and/or the university.

# CHAPTER 18

## Medical School and Beyond

*"You must be the change you wish to see in the world."*
—Gandhi

*"Those who bring sunshine to the lives of
others cannot keep it from themselves."*
—James Barrie

Congratulations! You have made it through high school, college, the MCAT, and the other hurdles necessary to make it to medical school. All that hard work and perseverance has paid off. Guess what? It isn't over yet. Medical school will probably be the toughest years of your life. No one said becoming a doctor was easy. First year medical students find themselves attending classes from 8 AM until 5 PM every day. The weekends are spent recovering or studying for upcoming exams.

Medical school is often viewed in two parts: "didactic" years in the classroom and "clinical" years doing rotations. The United States Medical Licensing Exam (USMLE) is given in three parts, and the first is given after the first two years of medical school.

Residency positions are based on test scores and class standing. In order to secure a competitive position in the field of your choice, you must continue to demonstrate your abilities. Once again, you must start from scratch and claw your way to the top! Here is some medical school advice that we received:

*Most seven year accelerated programs have a four-year medical school experience along with three years of college. The first two years of medical school are usually basic sciences (anatomy, histology, biochemistry, pathology, pharmacology, etc.). Learn your pathology and pharmacology well – it'll make your life easier on the wards.*

*This time is not too different from undergraduate courses. There is a course syllabus, selected readings, and labs. Here you will also learn how to do a physical exam, and several schools have you practice on model patients.*

*The last two years are usually clinical. This is when you do your rotations in the various core fields of medicine (internal medicine, pediatrics, family practice, surgery, etc). Life is usually pretty busy. You generally start early, (6-7am) and go until 5pm, or later if on call.*

*Standard textbooks are recommended—most of the learning is self-directed. At Boston University, there was a standard national test for each discipline that we would take. Usually we would use board review books to study. Be a sponge and soak everything up. Don't make hasty decisions about what field you want to go into because it looked glamorous on TV. Strive to do your best on each clinical rotation. It only makes the transition to residency easier.*

*Shuchi Gupta, MD*

This chapter was written by Drs. Jayakrishna Ambati & Balamurali K. Ambati. Balamurali holds the world's record as the youngest person to earn his or her medical degree. He graduated medical school before his eighteenth birthday.

## Introduction

When we were asked to write this chapter, we were both flattered and befuddled. It is a pleasure and a privilege to be asked to describe one's career to prospective high school students. We hope we can shed some insight on life in the world of medicine for you, the prospective doctors-to-be.

## The match program and residency

The final year of medical school is its easiest in terms of academics; its main objective is "the match," the day when medical students find out where they have gotten in for residency. It is easy to imagine throughout fourth year that once the match is over, one lives "happily ever after." Then July 1 happens, and the illusion of a fairy tale is quickly shattered.

July 1 is the standard day for internships, the first year of residency, to begin. If you thought medical school was hard, well, internship and residency make your whole life to date seem like a picnic. Very long hours, low pay, and even less respect make for a stressful time. Add to that the realization that just because you've gotten your MD doesn't mean you know how to be a doctor, and it's easy to become depressed or bitter.

But soon you realize that out of the depths of residency the doctor that is in you emerged. Self-confidence, and more importantly, competence soar; you actually *can* make people better. As you assume more responsibility for patients and you get your own interns and students, the experience becomes more fun. And then the cycle begins again. Residency ends, and you have to make new choices – do I go for more training in a fellowship; where should I work; should I stay academic or go into private practice? The magnitude of these choices dwarfs your previous ones, as these are choices for the rest of your life, not just a few years in residency. This is about where we are in our careers, so everything afterward is just speculation and observation.

## After residency

Once you finally finish your training, you are called an attending physician. No more courses to take, no more tests to pass, no more taking orders (hopefully). You have your own office and patients and responsibilities; no more safety net.

Doctors can practice and do many different things. There are countless specialties and subspecialties. Residency and fellowship can last anywhere from 3 to 10 years. After that, doctors can work full-time in a hospital, HMO, private office, or some combination. Some doctors devote much of their time to teaching or research; still others go into administration or business. One's patients can come from all ages in all walks of life, or one can be as exclusive as you wish. Some days are as exhilarating as "ER"; other days, you feel like a bureaucrat.

Finding the right position after training is finished is a difficult task. The major metropolitan areas where most doctors tend to want to live are already saturated, so pay is generally lower in the cities than in more remote areas in many specialties. Most doctors tend to join groups, to help ease costs of administration and call schedules. On average, doctors tend to work 65-70 hours a week; some surgeons work 80-90 hours a week, while doctors in other fields may have 9-5 jobs.

## Rewards of medicine

There is no generic "life of a doctor." But there are some common things that prospective students should know. Being a doctor is sometimes the most rewarding experience one can imagine: you save lives or vision, or give patients more time with their families. Other times, it just plain sucks: piles of paperwork, insurance companies, long hours can drive you insane. Many older doctors commonly complain that medicine isn't as fun as it used to be. But do not let the plaints of a disgruntled few dissuade you from medicine.

One should not strive to be a physician just to have a job, or even a career. Medicine is a calling. You can probably make more money more quickly for less work in professions like law, business, or technology. Yes, medicine has prestige and financial security, but those are of scarce comfort when you are awake at 3 in the morning.

Both of us chose to enter medicine for the opportunity to heal and the challenge of discovery. Our time in medicine has given us the chance to help people mend their wounds, see clearly, and come to terms with loss. It has presented us with challenges of fundamental biomedical questions that we can tackle head-on and hopefully unlock the door to future advances. It has helped us blossom into citizens capable of serving our community to our fullest.

In the brief time we have been doctors, we have witnessed a sea of changes in the practice of medicine. Managed care has made time a commodity and finances a pressing concern for all. It has eroded autonomy and corroded the patient-doctor bond. Still, our daily satisfaction has not diminished. Medicine *is* a wonderful field, but it asks, it demands, much of anyone who enters it.

The rewards of medicine are indeed great: essentially guaranteed financial security aside, the satisfaction of assuaging suffering and the daily intellectual challenge are unmatched by most other fields. But there is a steep price to pay in the pursuit of becoming a doctor, whether or not one succeeds in getting an MD.

Medical school and residency are a long and arduous road; almost all personal time is usurped by academic and clinical responsibilities. Debt and low pay weigh on the mind of almost every young doctor. Family life can be postponed indefinitely. For 7-14 years after college, the flower of youth has little time or money to experience life. Even after training is completed, doctors work longer hours than anyone else. There is a great toll this takes on families; in two-doctor households, it is all too common for children to not get the love and attention they need to prosper. This should not discourage kids from being doctors, but merely place things in perspective.

# Conclusion

Medicine is a divine calling and a great career, for those who are meant for it. The choice to enter it should at its core be a desire to heal, even at great personal sacrifice. To be sure, it is financially secure; to be honest, business and law are probably far more lucrative for the truly entrepreneurial. Not everyone has the right mix of scientific analytic skill, capacity for memorization, dedication, humanism, discipline, and guts that medicine requires. Just as well, there are better options than medicine for talented young people with other inclinations and capabilities.

So, we would like to conclude with a few tips:
1. Choose medicine if you genuinely care about making people better and making a difference. The intellectual and financial rewards are icing on the cake, but should not be the prime reason for becoming a doctor.
2. Once you do finish your training, make a critical choice: do you want to be a person who happens to be a doctor or a doctor who happens to be a person? Make sure you have priorities straight; it is all too easy to sacrifice yourself and more importantly your family to your career. If your family is a priority, then don't become a bigamist by letting your job become be-all and end-all, as it will come back to haunt you.
3. Being a good listener is the most important quality to be a good physician. Thoughtfulness, dedication, patience, kindness, and being a team player are the next most important traits (intelligence is a dime a dozen, and not as important as the above).
4. When you are so frustrated that you think you made the wrong choice (believe us, that time will come), think about the reasons you entered the field. If those are still true, you're OK.

5.  Never forget what it was like to be a student or resident;
    always respect and take care of those under your wing.

With a little luck and a lot of hard work, you will all do well.
All the best.

# CHAPTER 19

## Other Types of Accelerated and Combined Degree Programs

*"Sometimes I worry about being a success in a mediocre world."*
—Lily Tomlin

*"An ounce of hypocrisy is worth a pound of ambition."*
—Michael Korda

This chapter is about some alternative programs that you may consider applying to or just want to know more about. The first section talks about some types of medical programs other than the "typical" accelerated medical program that we've spent most of our time discussing. The second section deals with other accelerated programs within the medical field (dentistry, physical therapy, etc.), and the third section explains other ways to accelerate your education by getting multiple degrees, complementing your medical degree. There are accelerated programs in other non-medical fields as well, but those will not be discussed here.

## Other medical programs

### Eight-year programs
There are eight-year guaranteed medical programs available to high school students and much of the information provided in this book

applies to these programs. Eight-year programs are similar in their conditional acceptance, but obviously there is no acceleration. These programs would be geared towards students who want the full college experience but do not want to stress over medical school application later on.

**Early acceptance programs**
Some schools may offer accelerated medical programs through their affiliated medical school, but not for high school students. These are programs where college students may apply after their first or second year. If they are accepted, they have their route planned out for them. If not, they can still go pre-med traditionally.

# Accelerated dentistry and more

Accelerated medical programs are not for everyone because not everyone wants to be a doctor. There may be other accelerated programs that interest you if you still have the need for speed and reliability. These programs work parallel to medical programs in that you are still accepted from high school and go to college for a shortened period of time.

The difference is that these programs do not result in matriculation to medical school, but to dental school, physical therapy school, physician assistant school, podiatry school, etc.

These programs are not as recommended as medical programs, except to those who are absolutely certain about their future fields. The reason for this is that these programs will lead to more specific lines of work, while medical school is broader in career possibilities.

One student tells us why she applied to an accelerated physical therapy program, even though she still has lingering aspirations to attend medical school:

> *I am a biology and physical therapy major at Seton Hall University. It is a six-year program in which a BA in biology is*

*obtained in three years and the other three years are spent at UMDNJ for a Master's Degree in physical therapy. The requirements for this program are rather simple; once one makes the program they have to keep a 3.3 average and get nothing lower then a "C" in their science courses.*

*I never thought I wanted to become a doctor, but I came to SHU and did well in all of the science classes and worked as a student athletic trainer. That's when the idea of sports medicine entered my mind. I am now going to take the MCAT during my sophomore year and see how I do. This is a good plan because my options are still open to apply to medical school if I decide that's what is best for me.*

*Aleksandra Tamarkin*

Here is a piece written by a student in a combined accelerated dental program:

*I applied to colleges with the goal of becoming an orthodontist and getting into a dual degree program. As a senior in high school, this meant that I had double the amount of applications to do. I applied to a total of 22 colleges, half undergraduate and the other half accelerated dental programs. I was accepted into the Lehigh program affiliated with UPenn dental school.*

*I visited both campuses and loved them. I knew from the moment that I stepped on Lehigh's beautiful campus that I would definitely enroll there. The program is set up to be completed within seven years. My first three years are completed at Lehigh where I earn my Bachelor of Arts degree (BA). My admission to Penn depends upon multiple factors. I must have a 3.2 overall and science GPA, complete 90 hours, obtain a minimum score of 16 on the Dental Admission Test in all subject areas (out of 30), and have the determination and motivation needed to excel as a dentist. Furthermore, I must attend a final interview at Penn.*

*Now, I'm just beginning as a freshman in my spring semester. I attend classes like every other student and my major is biology (as declared by the program). I have a pre-professional advisor who helps me with all my problems. The program was the right decision for me. I recommend it to anyone who plans on working in the dental field. Guaranteed programs are great for people who know what profession they plan on entering. I will be out of dental school when I am twenty-five years old which is the average age of students entering dental school. So, I get a head start.*

*My experiences so far have been good. Obviously, the program is very rigorous and requires a lot of time and effort, but it is worth it. After all, in just about six years, I will have my DDS degree. I am very satisfied with my choice because I know that being a dentist will bring me nothing but happiness. The initial steps will be rough, but I know that I can conquer them.*

*Menka Malhotra*

## Graduate MD combined programs

Graduate medical programs are totally independent of accelerated BA/MD programs. They are for anyone in medical school, as long as that particular medical school offers them. Their relevance is that they are similar in scope to BA/MD programs, and usually people with that accelerated way of thinking would be interested in these programs as well.

Graduate MD combined programs are available through many of the medical schools affiliated with the BA/MD programs. Unfortunately, students coming through the accelerated route may have a harder time of being accepted. This is because of their younger age and the fact that their MCAT scores may not necessarily be as competitive because they were taken at a much earlier age. Strong candidates will not be discriminated against.

The graduate MD programs include getting a JD, PhD, MPH,

MBA, etc. Below is some information about MD/PhD programs written by an MD/PhD student at NYU:

**What exactly is an MD/PhD program?**
A certain number of US medical schools offer a combined degree program, which grants both MD and PhD degrees for individuals who wish to pursue medical research. The National Institute of Health's Medical Scientist Training Program (MSTP) may fund these programs. Essentially, the MD/PhD program is split into basic science years, research years, and clinical years.

The first two years of the program are identical to standard med. school years (students take the same classes with entering medical school classmates). The only difference within these first two years is that summers are spent doing research rotations—which involve doing small projects in labs of interest. After step 1 of the USMLE (which is taken at the end of year two), MD/PhD students will begin work in a research lab of their choice to conduct their thesis work.

The amount of time spent in pursuit of the PhD will vary with the lab you choose. On the average, this will be three or four years. After defending the thesis, students return to the clinical portion of med. school to complete their required clinical rotations and then do their electives (like 3rd and 4th year of "normal" med. school). After the program, students can continue by completing a post-doctorate, a residency or both!

**What are the requirements for acceptance to an MD/PhD program?**
You will want to have competitive GPA, competitive MCAT, good recommendations from research advisors (and non-science advisors) but most important is what kind of research you have done, and how well you can communicate it. Publications, abstracts, or anything of that sort is great. These programs are competitive—most schools allot about ten seats (sometimes more, sometimes less) per class.

**Why would someone want to be in this program?**
A student who is interested in medicine, but is particularly drawn to research may be interested in this program. Anyone who wants to go into academics (research, teaching), but wants a clinical training to provide different insights into research may also be interested.

**Pros and cons**
The advantages of participating in an MD/PhD program are that tuition is paid for, a stipend is given each year of the program, and there will be constant exposure to current research and workshops, seminars, etc. At the end of program, multiple options are available (even beyond residency and postdoctoral programs). MD/PhD's are highly favored by many residency programs and can get competitive residencies. The time it takes to get a PhD is usually shorter than it would be through traditional graduate programs (I didn't really list these in a very logical order, but you get the point).

The disadvantages include the fact that you have to invest a lot of time in pursuing both degrees—and we are not just talking about any seven or eight years. These are seven or eight years taken out of the prime of your life. Many of your peers will be established professionals by the time you take your qualifying exams. Even your medical school peers will be finished with residencies and beginning their own careers by the time you graduate. It will be hard to start a family if that's what you're looking at. Realistically, envision that you will be done with the program in your late twenties; you won't actually have a real "job" until mid-thirties.

# CHAPTER 20

## The Future of Medicine

*Next time you are being criticized for doing something a little
unusual, realize that there probably is a good reason that it
hasn't been done before—nobody ever thought of it.*
—Jason Yanofski

*There are three types of people; one lets things happen, one
hopes things happen, and one makes things happen.*
—Ashish Raju

Throughout this book we've shown you the ins and outs of accelerated medical programs. However, it is important to realize that medicine remains a dynamic entity in society. Deciding to practice medicine at a young age is a big commitment, as we've expressed. In this final chapter, we'll take a look at the bigger picture. The following piece is contributed by Dr. Judith Lasker, professor of sociology and author of *In Search of Parenthood; Coping with Infertility and High-Tech Conception* (1994).

> *Deciding whether or not to enter medicine as a career has
> become increasingly difficult, as dramatic changes have occurred
> in the practice of medicine in the United States. Physicians are
> challenged on every front, by patients who are both much more
> informed and more skeptical, by the threat of malpractice, by
> pressures and inducements from insurance and pharmaceutical*

*companies, by declining reimbursements, shorter visits, and constantly changing techniques and practices.*

*In the past, many students chose to become physicians because they could look forward to enjoying autonomy and independence in their work, as well as the possibility of helping others and the promise of high status and income. Today, one is almost certain to be employed by a corporation or to be part of a large practice group and to have almost every decision scrutinized and challenged by insurance companies. In the past, a physician most often took care of an entire family and knew them well; today, medical care is highly fragmented among a myriad of subspecialties.*

*The steadily increasing number of Americans without medical insurance, the complex problems posed by poverty, aging, and violence—all make the practice of medical care more and more difficult. And for the young, bright, and ambitious, there are alternatives to medical careers which offer the potential for even greater income, status, and autonomy without the many years of preparation. Is it any wonder that one physician threatened, not entirely in jest, to break his sons' legs if he entered medicine?*

*In spite of all the obstacles and discouragement, increasing numbers of Americans are applying to medical school, making the quest highly competitive. The field continues to offer constant intellectual challenge, prestige, and an opportunity to make a highly significant difference in the lives of many people. What else can match the possibility for improving and sometimes even saving human life?*

*And some of the changes in the practice of medicine have improved career experiences. No longer the almost exclusive domain of upper class white males, medicine offers greater opportunities than in the past for women and members of racial and ethnic minority groups. Corporate employment opens up the possibility of more regular hours and part-time employment, an advantage for parents who want to spend more time with their children. Reforms in medical education are preparing physicians better than in the past to deal with the challenges of communication, new ethical dilemmas, and cultural diversity.*

*The practice of medicine will continue to change in ways which cannot be fully anticipated. Discoveries in genetics, increased knowledge of alternative forms of healing, and the rapid aging of the population are just a few of the trends which are already influencing health care. Physicians also have an important role to play in promoting a healthier environment and in preventing the tragedies caused by a health system which is superb for some and unavailable for many others.*

*For those who are highly motivated to make a difference in the future world of medical care, and who are impatient to get started, this book provides very valuable information not readily available elsewhere. It describes the advantages and disadvantages of accelerated programs in a realistic and highly readable and personal fashion and offers a great deal of practical advice about such programs. Ashish and Jason are among those extraordinarily capable and motivated students who will make their mark in the medical field of the future. Writing this book while only in their second year of an accelerated program at Lehigh University, they have already started to do so.*

# A final note from the authors

We hope you enjoyed reading this book as much as we enjoyed writing it. Many months have been invested in providing you with nothing but the best advice and contributions from the most respected and renowned professionals and students. Looking at our completed project, we can honestly say that all our hard work has paid off, and we are proud of what we have accomplished.

Knowing that our book has helped you along that laborious journey "from high school to med. school" gives us a sense of great satisfaction. We've been with you since the beginning when you first considered the accelerated option. We've helped you make your high school years productive and taken you through the entire application process and much, much more.

One of the reasons that we decided to write such a book came from our own struggles at finding reliable information and advice. Fortunately, we did all right for ourselves, but that might not have been the case. In high school, we spent much time searching for a definitive guide but were unsuccessful – and so now we've taken some initiative and written it ourselves. The search is over!

When we began writing this book, we didn't expect it to be of this magnitude and scope. Because of our age and inexperience within the writing field, it was expected that we would face many obstacles. Many of these obstacles were annoying but short-lived, as we were persistent at moving towards other outlets until we were able to get what was needed for a specific chapter, etc.

As we began to make headway with our project, we were able to find contributors and obtain positive reviews, but most importantly, we gained support and respect. Now we are looking at convention presentations, newspaper interviews, and television appearances in our near future. The lesson that we have learned throughout this project is the same message that we hope has been a theme portrayed throughout the book: If you want something, you need to go after it, even if it isn't easy. If you keep this mentality, you *will* go far in life.

> *If you have to fight your way to the top, it*
> *will be especially worth it when you are in a*
> *position to sit back and enjoy the view.*
> —Jason Yanofski

# APPENDIX A

## Program Profiles and Rankings

### About program profiles and rankings

As prestigious as medical programs are, they have never been ranked systematically relative to each other. This is the first and *only* list of this kind. The following program rankings of combined degree BA/MD programs are based on five categories:

- Competitiveness
- Curriculum manageability/flexibility
- Quality of life
- Affordability
- Prestige of undergraduate/medical school

    Each category was given a rating of one to five stars (1 = worst/lowest, 5 = best/highest)

    Overall scores were then calculated based on how many stars each school was rated in total. The scores were then scaled so that the highest rated schools, which had 19 stars, received a total of 100. The individual category results can be seen in the school profiles, as well as the total scores. These profiles also contain contact information, program length etc.

### What do these rankings mean?

We ranked the top 15 schools based on their total scores, and listed schools that fell into our second tier. If you don't think that programs can be ranked because of their infinitely subtle qualities, then don't pay attention to this section. Some people, though, like this sort of thing!

Assigning stars to programs in the five categories was not an easy task, and much research and deliberating was done. The end result is an unbiased interpretation, but it may not be the only valid way to rank them.

What is important to do is to look at the factors that are important to you and only use those factors as a guide. For example, we included affordability as a factor because we felt that many students may have decided to apply to programs because of the financial benefit, and so this would be an important factor to them. On the other hand, another student may be less concerned with price and more focused on prestige, even if he isn't getting the best value for his buck.

This is also the case with quality of life. Many programs lost points because of the poor social environment provided by the undergraduate school. Though college years are shortened, they are still an important time. Again, some students will not feel the need to factor this in because their priorities are not the same.

The bottom line is that not everyone will use program profiles and rankings in the same way. Our overall scores do reflect our opinions as to what programs are more attractive, but they are only suggestions. Either way, this section should be a valuable reference in that you will be able to compare the programs relative to each other in a variety of aspects. You must contact schools directly to find out the latest developments in their curricula because things *will* change. Don't be hesitant in requesting brochures from all programs that you are interested in.

A final note is that though the programs are ranked relative to each other, *all* are competitive and prestigious. The caliber of each accelerated medical program is head and shoulders above most other academic routes. Even after our disclaimers, however, not everyone is going to be happy. The truth is that not all of the medical schools were cooperative, and because of that, their scores may not be reflective of everything that they have to offer. When information was scarce, we did our best to visit, research, and talk to students and faculty. If you think that your program deserves a second look or you would like to send us more information for the next edition, please contact us.

## Program profiles

# Program: Binghamton University

Contact Info: PO Box 6000, Binghamton, NY 13902-6000, phone: (607) 777-2000
Medical School Affiliation: SUNY Brooklyn College of Medicine
Contact Info: Health Science Center at Syracuse, P.O. Box 1000, Binghamton, NY 13902, phone: (607) 770-8618
Program Length: 8
Competitiveness: *
Curriculum manageability/flexibility: ****
Quality of life: ***
Affordability: *****
Prestige of undergraduate/medical school: **
Overall score: 84

# Program: Boston University

Contact Info: Associate Director, Admissions, 121 Bay State Road, Boston, MA 02215, phone: (617) 353-2330
Medical School Affiliation: Boston University School of Medicine
Program Length: 7-9 years
Competitiveness: ****
Curriculum manageability/flexibility: ****

Quality of life: ****
Affordability: *
Prestige of undergraduate/medical school: *****
Overall score: 92

# Program: Brooklyn College

Contact Info: Director of Admissions, Brooklyn College, 1602 James Hall, Brooklyn, NY 11210, phone: (718) 951-5044
Medical School Affiliation: SUNY Brooklyn College of Medicine
Program Length: 8
Competitiveness: ****
Curriculum manageability/flexibility: ***
Quality of life: *
Affordability: *****
Prestige of undergraduate/medical school: **
Overall score: 84

# Program: Brown University

Contact Info: Program in Liberal Medical Education Office, Box G-A134, Providence, RI 02912, phone: (401) 863-2450
Medical School Affiliation: Brown University School of Medicine
Program Length: 8 years
Competitiveness: *****
Curriculum manageability/flexibility: **
Quality of life: ****
Affordability: **
Prestige of undergraduate/medical school: *****
Overall score: 96

# Program: Case Western Reserve University

Pre-Professional Scholars Program
Contact Info: Office of Undergraduate Admission, 10900 Euclid Avenue, Cleveland, OH 44106-7055, phone: (216) 368-4450
Medical School Affiliation: Case Western Reserve University School of Medicine
Program Length: 8 years
Competitiveness: *****
Curriculum manageability/flexibility: ***
Quality of life: **
Affordability: **
Prestige of undergraduate/medical school: *****
Overall score: 92

# Program: The College of New Jersey

Contact Info: P.O. Box 7718, 2000 Pennington Rd., Ewing, NJ, 08628-0718, phone: (609) 771-1855
Medical School Affiliation: UMDNJ – New Jersey Medical School
Contact Info: Office of Admissions, C-653 MSB, 185 South Orange Avenue, Newark, NJ 07103-2714, phone: (201) 982-4631
Program Length: 7
Competitiveness: ***
Curriculum manageability/flexibility: ***
Quality of life: ***
Affordability: *****
Prestige of undergraduate/medical school: **
Overall score: 88

# Program: The College of William and Mary

Contact Info: P.O. Box 8795, Williamsburg, VA, 23187-8795, phone: (757) 221-4000
Medical School Affiliation: Eastern Virginia Medical School
Contact Info: 721 Fairfax Avenue, Norfolk, VA 23507-2000, phone: (804) 446-5812
Program Length: 8
Competitiveness: **
Curriculum manageability/flexibility: ***
Quality of life: *****
Affordability: ****
Prestige of undergraduate/medical school: **
Overall score: 88

# Program: Drew University

Contact Info: 36 Madison Ave, Madison, NJ, 07940, phone: (973) 408-3000
Medical School Affiliation: UMDNJ – New Jersey Medical School
Contact Info: Office of Admissions, C-653 MSB, 185 South Orange Avenue, Newark, NJ 07103-2714, phone: (201) 982-4631
Program Length: 7
Competitiveness: ***
Curriculum manageability/flexibility: ***
Quality of life: ***
Affordability: **
Prestige of undergraduate/medical school: ***
Overall score: 80

# Program: East Tennessee State University

Contact Info: Director, Premedical—Medical Program, Office of Medical Professions Advisement, P.O. Box 70,592, Johnson City, TN 37614-0592, phone: (615) 929-5602
Medical School Affiliation: East Tennessee State University James H. Quillen College of Medicine
Program Length: 8 years
Competitiveness: *
Curriculum manageability/flexibility: *****
Quality of life: **
Affordability: *****
Prestige of undergraduate/medical school: *
Overall score: 80

# Program: Fisk University

Contact Info: 1005 D.B. Todd, Jr. Boulevard, Nashville, TN 37208, phone: (615) 327-6425
Medical School Affiliation: Meharry Medical College
Program Length: 7
Competitiveness: ***
Curriculum manageability/flexibility: ***
Quality of life: **
Affordability: ****
Prestige of undergraduate/medical school: *
Overall score: 76

# Program: George Washington University

Contact Info: Office of Admissions, 2121 "I" Street, N.W., Washington, DC 20052, phone: (800) 447-3765
Medical School Affiliation: George Washington University School of Medicine
Program Length: 7 years
Competitiveness: ****
Curriculum manageability/flexibility: ***
Quality of life: ****
Affordability: *
Prestige of undergraduate/medical school: ***
Overall score: 84

# Program: Hampton University

Medical School Affiliation: Eastern Virginia Medical School
Contact Info: 721 Fairfax Avenue, Norfolk, VA 23507-2000, phone: (804) 446-5812
Program Length: 8
Competitiveness: ***
Curriculum manageability/flexibility: ***
Quality of life: **
Affordability: ***
Prestige of undergraduate/medical school: *
Overall score: 72

# Program: Howard University

Contact Info: Center for Preprofessional Education, P.O. Box 473, Administration Building, Washington, DC 20059, phone: (202) 806-7231

Medical School Affiliation: Howard University College of Medicine
Program Length: 8 years
Competitiveness: *
Curriculum manageability/flexibility: *****
Quality of life: **
Affordability: ****
Prestige of undergraduate/medical school: *
Overall score: 76

# Program: Illinois Institute of Technology

Contact Info: 10 West 33rd Street, Chicago, IL 60616, (312) 567-3025, phone: 1-800-448-2329
Medical School Affiliation: Finch University Health Sciences—Chicago Medical School
Contact Info: 3333 Green Bay Road, North Chicago, Illinois 60064-3095, phone: (847) 578-3000
Program Length: 8
Competitiveness: ****
Curriculum manageability/flexibility: ***
Quality of life: ***
Affordability: **
Prestige of undergraduate/medical school: **
Overall score: 80

# Program: Kent State University

Medical School Affiliation: Northeastern Ohio Universities College of Medicine

JASON YANOFSKI AND ASHISH RAJU

Contact Info: Associate Director of Admissions, 4209 State Route 44, P.O. Box 95, Rootstown, OH 44272-0095, phone: (216) 325-2511
Program Length: 6-7
Competitiveness: ***
Curriculum manageability/flexibility: ***
Quality of life: **
Affordability: ****
Prestige of undergraduate/medical school: *
Overall score: 76

# Program: Lehigh University

Contact Info: Office of Admissions, 27 Memorial Drive West, Bethlehem, PA 18105, phone: (610) 758-3100
Medical School Affiliation: MCP Hahnemann School of Medicine
Contact Info: 2900 Queen Lane, Philadelphia, PA 19129, phone: (215) 991-8100
Program Length: 6-7
Competitiveness: ****
Curriculum manageability/flexibility: ****
Quality of life: ****
Affordability: *
Prestige of undergraduate/medical school: ****
Overall score: 92

# Program: Michigan State University

Medical Scholars Program
Contact Info: Ann Arbor, MI 48109, phone: (734) 764-1817
Medical School Affiliation: Michigan State University College of Human Medicine
Contact Info: College of Human Medicine, Office of Admissions,

A-239 Life Sciences, East Lansing, MI 48824, phone: (517) 353-9620
Program Length: 8 years
Competitiveness: ***
Curriculum manageability/flexibility: ****
Quality of life: ***
Affordability: ***
Prestige of undergraduate/medical school: **
Overall score: 84

# Program: Montclair State University

Medical School Affiliation: UMDNJ – New Jersey Medical School
Contact Info: Office of Admissions, C-653 MSB, 185 South Orange Avenue, Newark, NJ 07103-2714, phone: (201) 982-4631
Program Length: 7
Competitiveness: ***
Curriculum manageability/flexibility: ***
Quality of life: *
Affordability: *****
Prestige of undergraduate/medical school: *
Overall score: 76

# Program: New Jersey Institute of Technology

Contact Info: University Heights, Newark, NJ 07102
Medical School Affiliation: UMDNJ – New Jersey Medical School
Contact Info: Office of Admissions, C-653 MSB, 185 South Orange Avenue, Newark, NJ 07103-2714, phone: (201) 982-4631
Program Length: 7
Competitiveness: ***
Curriculum manageability/flexibility: ****
Quality of life: ***

Affordability: \*\*\*\*
Prestige of undergraduate/medical school: \*\*
Overall score: 88

# Program: New York University

Contact Info: Admissions Office, College of Arts & Science, 22 Washington Square North, Room 904 Main Building, New York, NY 10003, phone: (212) 998-4500
Medical School Affiliation: New York University School of Medicine
Program Length: 8 years
Competitiveness: \*\*\*\*\*
Curriculum manageability/flexibility: \*\*\*
Quality of life: \*\*\*
Affordability: \*
Prestige of undergraduate/medical school: \*\*\*\*
Overall score: 88

# Program: Norfolk State University

Contact Info: 700 Park Avenue, Norfolk, VA 23504, phone: (757) 823-8600
Medical School Affiliation: Eastern Virginia Medical School
Contact Info: 721 Fairfax Avenue, Norfolk, VA 23507-2000, phone: (804) 446-5812
Program Length: 8
Competitiveness: \*\*\*
Curriculum manageability/flexibility: \*\*\*
Quality of life: \*\*
Affordability: \*\*\*\*
Prestige of undergraduate/medical school: \*
Overall score: 76

# Program: Northwestern University

Honors Program in Medical Education information
Contact Info: Office of Admission and Financial Aid, 1801 Hinman Avenue, Evanston, IL 60204-3060, phone: (708) 491-7271
Medical School Affiliation: Northwestern University Medical School
Program Length: 7 years
Competitiveness: ****
Curriculum manageability/flexibility: **
Quality of life: ******
Affordability: *
Prestige of undergraduate/medical school: *****
Overall score: 92

# Program: Old Dominion University

Contact Info: Hampton Boulevard, Norfolk, Virginia 23529, (757) 683-3000
Medical School Affiliation: Eastern Virginia Medical School
Contact Info: 721 Fairfax Avenue, Norfolk, VA 23507-2000, phone: (804) 446-5812
Program Length: 8
Competitiveness: **
Curriculum manageability/flexibility: ****
Quality of life: *
Affordability: *****
Prestige of undergraduate/medical school: *
Overall score: 76

# Program: Pennsylvania State University

Contact Info: Undergraduate Admissions, Pennsylvania State University, 201 Shields Building—Box 3000, University Park, PA 16802, phone: (814) 865-5471
Medical School Affiliation: Jefferson Medical College
Contact Info: 1020 Walnut Street, Philadelphia, PA 19107-5587, phone: (215) 955-6000
Program Length: 6
Competitiveness: *****
Curriculum manageability/flexibility: **
Quality of life: ****
Affordability: ***
Prestige of undergraduate/medical school: ****
Overall score: 96

# Program: Rensselaer Polytechnic Institute

Accelerated Biomedical Program
Contact Info: Admissions Counselor, Troy, NY 12180, phone: (518) 276-6216
Medical School Affiliation: Albany Medical College
Contact Info: 43 New Scotland Avenue, Albany, NY 12208, phone: (518) AMC-4302
Program Length: 6
Competitiveness: ****
Curriculum manageability/flexibility: ***
Quality of life: **
Affordability: **
Prestige of undergraduate/medical school: ***
Overall score: 80

# Program: Rice University

Contact Info: 6100 Main, Houston, Texas 77005 USA, (713) 348-0000
Medical School Affiliation: Baylor College of Medicine
Contact Info: Office of Admissions, One Baylor Plaza, Room 106A, Houston, TX 77030, phone: (713) 798-4841
Program Length: 8
Competitiveness: ****
Curriculum manageability/flexibility: ***
Quality of life: ****
Affordability: ***
Prestige of undergraduate/medical school: *****
Overall score: 100

# Program: Richard Stockton College of New Jersey

Contact Info: PO Box 195, Pomona, NJ 08240, phone: (609) 652-1776
Medical School Affiliation: UMDNJ – New Jersey Medical School
Contact Info: Office of Admissions, C-653 MSB, 185 South Orange Avenue, Newark, NJ 07103-2714, phone: (201) 982-4631
Program Length: 7
Competitiveness: ***
Curriculum manageability/flexibility: ***
Quality of life: *
Affordability: *****
Prestige of undergraduate/medical school: *
Overall score: 76

# Program: Rutgers University

Contact Info: P.O. Box 1059, Piscataway, NJ 08855-1059, (908) 445-5270
Medical School Affiliation: UMDNJ – Robert Wood Johnson Medical School
Contact Info: Office of Admissions, 675 Hoes Lane, Piscataway, NJ 08854, phone: (732) 235-4576.
Program Length: 8
Competitiveness: **
Curriculum manageability/flexibility: ***
Quality of life: **
Affordability: *****
Prestige of undergraduate/medical school: **
Overall score: 80

# Program: Siena College

Contact Info: Office of Admissions, Route 9, Loudonville, NY 12211, phone: (518) 783-2423
Medical School Affiliation: Albany Medical College
Contact Info: 43 New Scotland Avenue, Albany, NY 12208, phone: (518) AMC-4302
Program Length: 8
Competitiveness: ****
Curriculum manageability/flexibility: ****
Quality of life: ***
Affordability: **
Prestige of undergraduate/medical school: **
Overall score: 84

# Program: Sophie Davis School of Biomedical Education

Contact Info: Y Building, Room 705N, 138th Street & Convent Avenue, New York, NY 10031, phone: (212) 650-7707
Medical School Affiliation: City University of New York Medical School
Program Length: 7
Competitiveness: ***
Curriculum manageability/flexibility: ***
Quality of life: *
Affordability: *****
Prestige of undergraduate/medical school: *
Overall score: 76

# Program: Stevens Institute of Technology

Contact Info: Hoboken, NJ 07102, phone: (201) 216-5000
Medical School Affiliation: UMDNJ – New Jersey Medical School
Contact Info: Office of Admissions, C-653 MSB, 185 South Orange Avenue, Newark, NJ 07103-2714, phone: (201) 982-4631
Program Length: 7
Competitiveness: ***
Curriculum manageability/flexibility: ***
Quality of life: ***
Affordability: **
Prestige of undergraduate/medical school: ***
Overall score: 80

# Program: Union College

Contact Info: Associate Dean of Admissions, Union College, Schenectady, NY 12308, phone: (518) 388-6112
Medical School Affiliation: Albany Medical College
Contact Info: 43 New Scotland Avenue, Albany, NY 12208, phone: (518) AMC-4302
Program Length: 8
Competitiveness: ****
Curriculum manageability/flexibility: ***
Quality of life: ***
Affordability: ***
Prestige of undergraduate/medical school: ***
Overall score: 88

# Program: University of Akron

Contact Info: 302 E. Buchtel Mall, Akron, Ohio 44325
Medical School Affiliation: Northeastern Ohio Universities College of Medicine
Contact Info: Associate Director of Admissions, 4209 State Route 44, P.O. Box 95, Rootstown, OH 44272-0095, phone: (216) 325-2511
Program Length: 6-7
Competitiveness: ***
Curriculum manageability/flexibility: ***
Quality of life: *
Affordability: *****
Prestige of undergraduate/medical school: *
Overall score: 76

# Program: University of Alabama

Medical School Affiliation: University of Alabama School of Medicine
Contact Info: Medical Student Services, VH P-100, 1530 3rd Avenue S, Birmingham AL 35294-0019, phone: (205) 934-2330
Program Length: 7-9
Competitiveness: ***
Curriculum manageability/flexibility: ****
Quality of life: ***
Affordability: ****
Prestige of undergraduate/medical school: **
Overall score: 88

# Program: University of California Riverside

Contact Info: Division of Biomedical Sciences, Riverside, CA 92521-0121, phone: (909) 787-4333
Medical School Affiliation: UCLA School of Medicine
Program Length: 7
Competitiveness: **
Curriculum manageability/flexibility: ***
Quality of life: **
Affordability: *****
Prestige of undergraduate/medical school: ****
Overall score: 88

# Program: University of Miami

Contact Info: Coral Gables, Florida 33124, phone: (305) 284-2211
Medical School Affiliation: University of Miami School of Medicine
Program Length: 7
Competitiveness: ***
Curriculum manageability/flexibility: ****
Quality of life: *****
Affordability: *
Prestige of undergraduate/medical school: ***
Overall score: 88


# Program: University of Michigan

Interflex Program
Contact Info: 5113 Medical Science I Building, Wing C, Ann Arbor, MI 48109-0611, phone: (313) 764-9534
Medical School Affiliation: University of Michigan Medical School
Program Length: 8 years
Competitiveness: ***
Curriculum manageability/flexibility: ****
Quality of life: ***
Affordability: ***
Prestige of undergraduate/medical school: ***
Overall score: 88


# Program: University of Missouri – Kansas City

Contact Info: 5100 Rockhill Road, Kansas City MO 64110-2499, phone: (816) 235-1000

Medical School Affiliation: University of Missouri – Kansas City
School of Medicine
Contact Info: School of Medicine, Council on Selection, 2411
Holmes, Kansas City, MO 64108, phone: (816) 235-1870
Program Length: 6 years
Competitiveness: ***
Curriculum manageability/flexibility: **
Quality of life: **
Affordability: ***
Prestige of undergraduate/medical school: **
Overall score: 72

# Program: University of Rochester

Rochester Early Medical Scholars
Contact Info: Meliora Hall, Rochester, NY 14627, phone: (716)
275-3221
Medical School Affiliation: University of Rochester School of Medi-
cine and Dentistry
Program Length: 8 years
Competitiveness: *****
Curriculum manageability/flexibility: ***
Quality of life: ***
Affordability: **
Prestige of undergraduate/medical school: *****
Overall score: 96

# Program: University of South Alabama

Contact Info: Mobile AL 36688-0002, phone: (334) 460-6101
Medical School Affiliation: University of South Alabama College
of Medicine
Program Length: 8 years

Competitiveness: **
Curriculum manageability/flexibility: ****
Quality of life: **
Affordability: ****
Prestige of undergraduate/medical school: *
Overall score: 76

# Program: University of Southern California

Contact Info: University Park Campus, Los Angeles, California 90089, phone: (213) 740-2311
Medical School Affiliation: University of Southern California School of Medicine
Program Length: 7 years
Competitiveness: ***
Curriculum manageability/flexibility: ***
Quality of life: ****
Affordability: *
Prestige of undergraduate/medical school: ***
Overall score: 80

# Program: University of Wisconsin

Medical Scholars Program
Contact Info: 1300 University Avenue, Room 1250, Madison, WI 53706, phone: (608) 263-7561
Medical School Affiliation: University of Wisconsin – Madison Medical School
Program Length: 7-9 years
Competitiveness: **
Curriculum manageability/flexibility: ****
Quality of life: ***

Affordability: ****
Prestige of undergraduate/medical school: ****
Overall score: 92

# Program: Villanova University

Contact Info: Office of Undergraduate Admissions, 800 Lancaster Avenue, Villanova, PA 19085-1699, phone: 1-800-338-7927
Medical School Affiliation: MCP Hahnemann School of Medicine
Contact Info: 2900 Queen Lane, Philadelphia, PA 19129, phone: (215) 991-8100
Program Length: 6-7
Competitiveness: ****
Curriculum manageability/flexibility: ***
Quality of life: ****
Affordability: **
Prestige of undergraduate/medical school: ***
Overall score: 88

# Program: Youngstown State University

Contact Info: One University Plaza, Youngstown, OH 44555
Medical School Affiliation: Northeastern Ohio Universities College of Medicine
Contact Info: Associate Director of Admissions, 4209 State Route 44, P.O. Box 95, Rootstown, OH 44272-0095, phone: (216) 325-2511
Program Length: 6-7
Competitiveness: ***
Curriculum manageability/flexibility: ****
Quality of life: *
Affordability: *****
Prestige of undergraduate/medical school: *
Overall score: 80

# Combined Degree Program Rankings

## Top 15 Combined Degree Programs (Tier I)
1. Rice University
2. Brown University
3. Penn State University
4. University of Rochester
5. Case Western Reserve University
6. Northwestern University
7. Lehigh University
8. Boston University
9. University of Wisconsin
10. New York University
11. University of California – Riverside
12. Villanova University
13. College of New Jersey
14. University of Michigan
15. University of Miami

## Tier II (Listed alphabetically)
Brooklyn College
Binghamton University
College of William and Mary
George Washington University
Michigan State University
New Jersey Institute of Technology
Rensselaer Polytechnic Institute
Siena College
Union College
University of Alabama

# Programs Listed by Length

## 6 years
Pennsylvania State University
Rensselaer Polytechnic Institute
University of Missouri – Kansas City

## 6-7 years
Kent State University
Lehigh University
University of Akron
Villanova University
Youngstown State University

## 7 years
The College of New Jersey
Drew University
Fisk University
George Washington University
Montclair State University
New Jersey Institute of Technology
Northwestern University
Richard Stockton College of New Jersey
Sophie Davis School of Biomedical Education
Stevens Institute of Technology
University of California Riverside
University of Miami
University of Southern California

## 7-9 years
Boston University
University of Alabama
University of Wisconsin

**8 years**

> Binghamton University
> Brooklyn College
> Brown University
> Case Western Reserve University
> The College of William and Mary
> East Tennessee State University
> Hampton University
> Howard University
> Illinois Institute of Technology
> Michigan State University
> New York University
> Norfolk State University
> Old Dominion University
> Rice University
> Rutgers University
> Siena College
> Union College
> University of Michigan
> University of Rochester
> University of South Alabama

# Programs Listed by State

**Alabama**
University of Alabama
University of South Alabama

**California**
University of California Riverside
University of Southern California

**Washington, D.C.**
George Washington University
Howard University

**Florida**
University of Miami

**Illinois**
Illinois Institute of Technology
Northwestern University

**Massachusetts**
Boston University

**Michigan**
Michigan State University
University of Michigan

**Missouri**
University of Missouri – Kansas City

**New Jersey**
The College of New Jersey
Drew University
Montclair State University

New Jersey Institute of Technology
Richard Stockton College of New Jersey
Rutgers University
Stevens Institute of Technology

## New York
Binghamton University
Brooklyn College
New York University
Rensselaer Polytechnic Institute
Siena College
Sophie Davis School of Biomedical Education
Union College
University of Rochester

## Ohio
Case Western Reserve University
Kent State University
University of Akron
Youngstown State University

## Pennsylvania
Lehigh University
Pennsylvania State University
Villanova University

## Rhode Island
Brown University

## Tennessee
East Tennessee State University
Fisk University

## Texas
Rice University

**Virginia**
   The College of William and Mary
   Hampton University
   Norfolk State University
   Old Dominion University

**Wisconsin**
   University of Wisconsin

# APPENDIX B

## Research on Combined Degree and Accelerated Medical Programs

While writing this book, we recognized that background information on accelerated medical programs was necessary for you to make informed decisions. With that in mind, we decided to find out as much information as possible about their history. Through this investigation, we discovered that over the past forty years, several studies were performed and research articles were written. In this appendix, we have provided citations to some key articles on accelerated programs. Following each citation we provide a brief summary that should help you understand the scope and purpose of each article. We highly recommend that you obtain and read these articles on your own in order to make an informed decision on whether or not accelerated medical programs are for you.

All of the articles we have read are from *Academic Medicine*. This is the journal of the American Association of Medical College (AAMC). This publication is not common to most libraries. You may have to go to a hospital or larger library to get a copy of these articles. Happy hunting! If you are not of the hunting variety, we have included the full text of one particularly relevant article (Albanese, et. al) at the end of the appendix.

Albanese M., Vaneyck S., Huggett K., Barnet JH., "Academic performances of early-admission students to a BA/MD program compared with regular-admission students in relation to applicant pool fluctuations." *Academic Medicine*, 72(No.10/Supplement 1): S66-8, October 1997.

In this recent article, Albanese and fellow researchers "determine how BA/MD students' academic performances compared with those of regular students in relationship to the numbers of applicants to a medical school over the ten year period from 1986 to 1995." The program used to conduct the research was the BA/MD program at the University of Wisconsin. This study is similar to the Jefferson Penn State study in that various "measures of academic performance" were utilized and it was specific to one program. The article states, "These results suggest that a BA/MD program that uses high standards of academic performance in high school for admission can have a buffering effect on the quality of students admitted to medical school in periods of low applicant pools." The article continues and later states, "In periods of large applicant pools, the BA/MD students performed equally as well as the regular students, suggesting that there was no 'rebound' penalty for having a BA/MD program." The researchers are careful to mention that their findings "generalize to a limited number of BA/MD programs." This is of course because there are inherent variations from program to program. Nevertheless, the researchers appear to support accelerated medical programs. "The BA/MD programs have withstood the test of time in terms of enrolling students who perform as well or better than their regularly admitted peers."

Arnold L., Xu G., Epstein LC., Jones B., "Professional and personal characteristics of graduates as outcomes of differences between combined baccalaureate—MD degree programs." *Academic Medicine*, 71(No.1/Supplement): S64-6, January 1996.

This research article's main goal was to identify variations of the curricula and program length to determine the effect on students that have completed combined degree programs. Not every combined degree program is the same. Some emphasize a liberal arts education, while others are very medicine specific. Some programs are six or seven years, while others are eight years in duration. Arnold and his colleagues collected responses using a survey method and discovered that "relatively few differences in graduates' professional and personal characteristics were associated with the type of CD program attended." It continues, "typically, the main effect of the program length accounted for the differences." They found that 6-year programmers were proficient in "clinical knowledge and skills" and "were most often engaged in the private practice of medicine in clinical settings." 7 or 8-year programmers "were especially well prepared in the basic sciences and self-education skills. They were a little more likely to be in academic or salaried positions, or still in training." Arnold engenders an interesting point of "doctors as clinicians" versus "doctors as scholars." It appears that 6-year programmers were more clinically oriented, while 7 or 8-year programmers were more scholarly oriented.

Callahan C., Veloski JJ., Xu G., Hojat M., Zeleznik C., Gonnella JS., "The Jefferson-Penn State B.S.-M.D. program: a 26-year experience." *Academic Medicine,* 67(No. 11): 792-7, November 1992.

This very comprehensive study follows students of the Jefferson-Penn State BS/MD program from 1964-1989. This article states that, "the major factors that encouraged the development of these programs included a shortage of physicians; a desire to eliminate the overlap between the baccalaureate and medical curricula; an attempt to reduce the cost of a medical education for both students and colleges; and a desire to attract the academically talented student who might have been lost to medicine because of the length of time involved to earn a medical degree." This "study was designed to examine the premedical, medical, and postgraduate performances of students in the accelerated program compared with those students in the usual eight-year curriculum, over a 26-year period." The researchers believed that combined degree students would perform as well as other highly qualified students. This was a very in depth study that utilized GPA's, USMLE scores, junior written examinations, among many other "performance factors." What did the researchers find? Their "hypothesis that the accelerated and control groups would perform equally well in medical school was largely confirmed." The control group had superior records and showed academic excellence. The researchers therefore concluded that, "the similarity of accelerated and control groups during and after medical school can be considered an especially strong indication of the success of the accelerated students." There are individuals in the medical community who believe that accelerated medical programs should not exist. This Jefferson-Penn State research article contradicts their beliefs.

**Norman AW, Calkins EV., "Curricular variations in combined baccalaureate-M.D. programs."** *Academic Medicine,* 67(No. 11): 785-91, November 1992.

If you are interested in finding out the goals and history of accelerated medical programs, this is the article to get your hands on. The authors in this research paper cover various aspects of different programs across the US. It is interesting to note that the goals of various programs differ. Some exist to offer "early acceptance to medical school." Others want "to train primary care physicians" and "to prepare well-trained doctors for community medicine." In our book, we have shown that variations do exist between programs. The authors echo our message in their discussion. "No two of the 34 programs are alike. They differ in length, number of students, curricular goals and emphasis, type of baccalaureate degree, special features, and the number of institutions of higher education involved." Please refer to Appendix A to see a more detailed analysis of the programs available today.

Olson SW., "Combined-degree Programs: a valuable alternative for motivated students who choose medicine early." *Academic Medicine,* 67(No. 11): 783-84, November 1992.

Dr. Olson discusses the background of combined degree programs in this article. If you compare citations, you will notice that this article was cited in the article entitled, "Curricular variations in combined baccalaureate-M.D. programs." That particular issue of *Academic Medicine* highlighted combined degree programs in detail. This article by Olson is often referred to by more recent. Olson states, "The more favorable results reported in this issue of *Academic Medicine* suggest that more institutions could beneficially establish combined degree programs."

## Conclusion

There are many interesting trends that can be realized about accelerated medical programs by the literature provided.

1.  The **purpose** of each program varies widely and each program retains a uniqueness of its own. The purposes of these programs include selecting medical doctors at a young age, training doctors that will work in under-represented areas, providing a more "liberal" education to future physicians, and increasing the quality of a low applicant pool.
2.  Due to differing goals, **variations in length, curriculum, etc.** exist between each program.
3.  Because of these differences, physicians from different programs do exhibit differences in attitude.
4.  Despite the aforementioned differences, many studies have strongly correlated **high levels of performance** with students going through these programs. "Combined degree students perform as well and at times better than the average medical student," appears to be a reoccurring statement.

5. There are obviously individuals who question the integrity of accelerated programs. That is probably why there continues to be **reevaluations** every few years to the quality and performance of individuals involved in these programs.

Reprinted with permission. Data tables and figures have been omitted.

## Academic Performances of Early-admission Students to a BA/MD Program Compared with Regular-admission Students in Relation to Applicant Pool Fluctuations

### MARK ALBANESE, SELMA VANEYCK, KATIE HUGGETT, and JODI H. BARNET

BA/MD programs have been in existence for almost 40 years. Numerous studies of comparisons of admits to these programs (admitted upon graduation from high school) to regular medical school admits have found that BA/MD students perform as well or better.[1] A recent study, which controlled for the high level of academic performance required for admittance to a BA/MD program, found that the performance of BA/MD students and high-ability regular students were generally indistinguishable.[2] One potential benefit of a BA/MD program may be to moderate the influence of declines in applicant pools on the quality of matriculating medical students. In the period 1987 to 1990, the applicants to US medical schools dropped below 30,000, reaching historical lows. With the decline in the applicant pool, undergraduate grade-point averages (GPAs) suffered commensurate reductions, reaching a low of 3.40 in 1989, when the number of applicants was only 26,915 (in 1995, for example, the applicant pool was 46,591 and the matriculating GPAs were 3.51). While undergraduate GPAs are one measure of the class quality, a more important concern is whether performance in medical school and on licensure examinations show comparable fluctuations with the changes in the number of medical school applicants. In the present study we determined how BA/MD students' academic performances compared with those of regular students in relationship to the numbers of applicants to a medical school over the ten-year period 1986 to 1995.

## Method

The BA/MD program at the University of Wisconsin Medical School has been in existence since 1981. Since its inception, the number of students admitted has increased from 10 in 1984 to 50 in 1996. Students are admitted to the program upon graduation from high school. To be competitive for the program, students must have a combined American College Test (ACT) score of at least 30, or a Scholastic Aptitude Test score of at least 1360, or be in the top 5% of their graduating high school classes and have a GPA of at least 3.8/4.0. For the 1996 admitting class, the average ACT score was 32.5. The BA/MD program students do not have to take the Medical College Admission Test, but they must maintain at least a 3.0 GPA overall and either a 3.6 in science/math or 3.2 in advanced science/math.

Three sets of academic performance measures were used to compare BA/MD with regular students: undergraduate GPAs, medical school grades over the first three years, and National Board of Medical Examiners/US Medical Licensing Examination scores. Effect sizes were computed for each academic measure by subtracting regular students' mean scores from BA/MD students' scores and dividing by the standard deviation of the regular students' scores. Separate effect sizes were computed for each of the ten entering classes over the ten-year period. (Converting scores to effect sizes within class overcomes some of the scaling problems inherent in measures that evolve and change over time.)

Two-tailed t-tests were used to test effect sizes for statistical significance. To examine the relationship between effect sizes and applicant pool numbers, Spearman rank-order correlations were computed. For the years during which the national applicant pool dropped below 30,000, effect sizes were averaged and compared with the average effect sizes in the six years when the national applicant pool exceeded 30,000.

## Results

Table 1 shows the effect sizes and their statistical significance for each year and each measure. Positive effect-size values indicate that the BA/MD students had higher scores than did the regular students, and vice versa. In the far right column, Spearman rank-order correlations are shown. The correlation between the national applicant pool and the mean matriculating GPA was .84, quantifying the extent to which the GPAs of matriculating medical students declined as the applicant pool declined (and vice versa).

The correlations of the effect sizes for the local measures with the national applicant pool showed negative relationships, with correlations ranging from -.60 to -.77. The negative correlation of effect sizes with the numbers in the applicant pool indicates that as the number of applicants dropped, the BA/MD students outperformed their regular admit peers by an increasing margin. The relationships were strongest for first- and third-year medical school GPAs, which were statistically significant at the .01 and .05 margin, respectively, and accounted for almost 60% of the variability in scores.

Table 2 shows the mean effect sizes for the "trough" years, when the applicant pool dropped below 30,000, compared with the means for the years in which the applicant pool exceeded 30,000. This comparison magnifies the effect of the BA/MD program by focusing on the years when the applicant pool was at its very smallest. The effect sizes were all in the direction of demonstrating greater BA/MD student performances differentials during the trough years compared with the other years. The differentials were greatest for the licensure examination scores, with effect sizes during the trough years over 0.5 SD greater than during the nontrough years.

## Discussion

These results suggest that a BA/MD program that uses high standards of academic performance in high school for admission can have a buffering effect on the quality of students admitted to medical school in periods of low applicant pools. The program has its greatest buffering effect over the ten-year period under study, when the applicant pool dropped below 30,000. The maximum effect on student performance occurred during 1988, the year when the applicant pool was at its nadir. In periods of large applicant pools, the BA/MD students performed equally as well as the regular students, suggesting that there was no "rebound" penalty for having a BA/MD program.

Using the 30,000 threshold as an indicator of when a BA/MD program becomes a buffer is predicated upon several factors. First, the threshold is dependent upon the number of positions available in medical school. If there should be a significant decline in the number of positions available, the buffering may not occur until the applicant pool reached even lower levels. Second, the threshold is dependent upon the medicine's continuing to attract the "best and the brightest." If the field should happen to become less attractive to these students, a BA/MD program could provide a buffer even if there were an increase in the number of applicants. A BA/MD program gives students who are interested in a career in medicine a "path of least resistance," which may keep some students on a trajectory to medical school even in the presence of general declining interest.

One might consider waiting to start a BA/MD program until there is solid evidence that a decline in the applicant pool is occurring. The problem with this approach is that it takes three to four years until students admitted to the BA/MD program enter medical school and it also takes time to gain awareness of the program by high school counselors and others necessary to make such a program work. In early years of development, the quality of students who apply may not be as great as desired. Thus, such a strategic approach to developing a BA/MD program is not likely to be successful.

A methodological issue that should be discussed is why we used numbers from the national rather than the local applicant pool. The main reason was that the way in which out-of-state resident applications were handled at our institution changed radically during the period in which the number of applicants declined. At the beginning of the period we analyzed, request from out-of-state residents for applications were turned down. As the reduction in the applicant pool became more severe, a decision was made to send out applications to all students regardless of state of residency. It also was not clear from the records kept during this period whether the numbers reflected the number of students requesting applications or the number of completed applications received. For these reasons, we believed the national applicant pool reflected a more accurate assessment of the "true" number of applicants.

A BA/MD program does have a cost. For our program, there is a direct cost for a .4 full-time equivalent (FTE) program director, .5 FTE graduate assistant, recruitment expenses, and expenses for some programming for the students during their undergraduate years. A generous estimate of the current costs for our program is $50,000. There is an additional cost of $1,500 per student for student stipends for summer research work. An indirect cost is incurred by the increased burden for the admissions committee to review applications for the program. There is also intangible cost incurred because some people feel that the admission process for the BA/MD program is unfair compared with the regular admit process because program students have not had to suffer the competition for undergraduate grades and take the MCAT.

It is important to point out that the results from our program only generalize to a limited number of BA/MD programs. Some BA/MD programs are accelerated, leading to the MD degree in six years. Other BA/MD programs encompass the entire entering medical school class. In comparison, our program is very limited. Additional research will be needed to determine whether our results generalize to these other types of BA/MD programs.

As the health care environment continues to be restructured and resources become increasingly scarce, all programs that medical schools offer will be scrutinized for their value. The BA/MD programs have withstood the test of time in terms of enrolling students who perform as well or better than their regularly admitted peers. These programs may also give students the freedom to take a broader balance of courses in the natural and the social sciences and in the humanities as undergraduates, one of the major reasons why the program was developed at our institution and a recommendation of the Project Panel on the General Education of the Physician and College Preparation for Medicine (conclusion 2, recommendation 1).[3] Other reasons include to relieve students from the pressures of undergraduate grade competition and to eliminate the sharp distinction between undergraduates and medical education. In a recent survey of our graduates, there was overwhelming agreement that all three of these goals were met. This study suggests that such a BA/MD program may have the added benefit of bolstering the quality of the medical school matriculants in times of low-applicant pools.

Correspondence: Mark A. Albanese, PhD, Director, Medical Education Research and Development, University of Wisconsin Medical School, 2070 Medical Sciences Center, 1300 University Avenue, Madison, WI 53706-1532.
e-mail: <mark.albanese@mail.admin.wisc.edu>

## References

1. Olson SW. Combined degree programs: a valuable alternative for motivated students who choose medicine early. Acad Med. 1992;67:783-4.

2. Callahan C, Veloski JJ, Xu G, Hojat M, Zeleznik C, Gonnella JS. The Jefferson-Penn State BS-MD program: a 26-year experience. Acad Med. 1992;67:792-7.
3. Muller S (chair). Physicians for the twenty-first century: report of the Project Panel on the General Education of the Physician and College Preparation for Medicine. J Med Educ. 1984;59.

# APPENDIX C

## Listing of Summer Programs

In Chapter Five, we stressed the importance of summer programs. Here, David Reibstein, founder of the Penn Summer Science Academy provides the introduction to this appendix, followed by short descriptions of some summer programs provided by the program directors.

*High school students interested in pursuing a career in science, math, engineering or medicine are well advised to involve themselves in related activities well before college. These fields are very competitive, and you will want to distinguish yourself from the many others who have academic records just as good as yours. One of the most important ways is to engage in science-related activities outside your regular schoolwork. Doing research or being in a program that puts you in contact with research are two very good ways to convince others of your seriousness and enable you to learn whether you are suited for this kind of career.*

*Many universities and colleges offer summer programs for high school students interested in science. Some offer an opportunity to take advanced courses. While this is undoubtedly helpful, and may be just what you want, taking a regular college-level course is not going to give you that research experience or exposure. For that, you should look for a program, almost always non-credit, that provides research or something close to it.*

*One example is the Penn Summer Science Academy at the*

University of Pennsylvania (http://www.sas.upenn.edu/CGS/ highschool/pssa.shtml). PSSA is a non-credit program consisting of both guided and independent laboratory projects, seminars, workshops, faculty lectures, discussion groups, and problem-solving sessions, all taught by Penn scientists and students.

Similar programs are conducted at many major research universities and some smaller college. One resource for finding these is the organization Science Service. At their web site—http://www.sciserv.org/stp/—you will find a searchable directory of what they call "Science Training Programs." However, listings are by no means complete and up to date, and include only those programs that have submitted their descriptions.

Another listing is maintained by the National Science Foundation (NSF) at http://www.ehr.nsf.gov/ehr/esie/ studentops.html but many of these listing are out of date and the list is very far from complete. You should contact each program listed there to find out if it is still functioning.

You can do a more thorough search by going to the web site of each college that may interest you and searching for the information yourself. Often such programs may be found within individual science departments, or in a Continuing Education or Special Programs division. Most university web sites have a search utility.

Also consider the Governors' Schools conducted by about 35 states. See the National Conference of Governors' Schools site at http://www-pgss.mcs.cmu.edu/NCoGS/

These programs vary a great deal in the kinds of activities, size, location, etc, and you'll probably find one you like. Some are free, some charge fees, and some of the latter give financial aid. These programs will not only give you a leg up in your science/medicine career, they'll give you a chance to experience a little of college life.

Dr. David Reibstein founded the Penn Summer Science Academy. He is now Outreach Director at the Princeton Materials Institute.

He may be reached by email at dr@princeton.edu or by phone at (609) 258-5598; his web page is www.princeton.edu/~dr

## Boston University
## Program In Mathematics For Young Scientists (PROMYS)

PROMYS offers a lively mathematical environment in which ambitious high school students explore the creative world of mathematics. Through their intensive efforts to solve a large assortment of unusually challenging problems in Number theory, the participants practice the art of mathematical discovery—numerical exploration, formulation and critique of conjectures, and techniques of proof and generalization. More experienced participants may also study algorithms, geometry and topology, or combinatorics. Problem sets are accompanied by daily lectures given by research mathematicians with extensive experience in Professor Arnold Ross's long-standing Summer Mathematics Program at Ohio State University. In addition, a highly competent staff of 15 college-aged counselors lives in the dormitories and is always available to discuss mathematics with students. Each participant will meet with professional mathematicians several times per week for problem-solving and open-ended explorations. Special lectures by outside speakers offer a broad view of mathematics and its role in the sciences.

PROMYS is a residential program designed for 60 ambitious high school students entering grades 10 through 12. Admission decisions will be based on the following criteria: applicants' solutions to a set of challenging problems included with the application packet; teacher recommendations; high school transcripts; and student essays explaining their interest in the program.

Cost: The approximate cost of room and board is $1400. Books may cost an additional $100. There is no cost to students for tuition thanks to the support of our sponsors. Financial aid is available. PROMYS is dedicated to the principle that no student will be unable to attend because of financial need.

PROMYS is directed by Professor Glenn Stevens. Applications

will be available in February and accepted from March 1 until June 1, 2000 and can be obtained by writing to:

PROMYS
Department of Mathematics
Boston University
111 Cummington Street
Boston, MA 02215
Phone: (617) 353-2563
E-mail at promys@math.bu.edu
Web: http://math.bu.edu/people/promys

## Northwestern University
## Center for Talent Development

Center for Talent Development offers three-week summer sessions for talented adolescents. Students either commute to class or live in a residential dormitory during these intensive classes, which run 5 hours a day, 5 days a week. Classes are held on the campus of Northwestern University, a major research institution. Age-appropriate supervision and residential activities, including excursions throughout the Chicago area, are provided. Grades are awarded and high school credit is granted for successful completion of courses. Courses include a range of subjects in math, science, humanities, and the social sciences. Relevant courses for pre-med students include Honors Biology, Honors Chemistry, Human Biology, Recombinant DNA and Biotechnology, Scientific Research Methods, and math courses from Algebra through Topics in Calculus.
Contact:

Summer Program Director
Center for Talent Development
Northwestern University
617 Dartmouth Place
Evanston, IL 60208 phone: 847-491-3782 fax: 847-467-4283
email: ctd@nwu.edu

Web: http://www.ctd.nwu.edu

## University of California

The University of California Riverside's Summer Academy is an opportunity for high school students to take an introductory university course at the campus during the summer. The Summer Academy is offered in two accelerated five-week sessions from late June or early July, and late July through early September. Students who successfully complete the Summer Academy will earn full University of California, Riverside credit and grades, which apply to a UC degree. We offer introductory courses in the arts, humanities, mathematics, sciences, and the social sciences. Students attend class with regular UCR students and students from other college campuses. This credit is often transferable to institutions outside of the UC system. As part of the experience, the Summer Academy also offers programs and field trips during the first Session designed to enhance the Academy students' summer at UCR. We are seeking students who have completed the 9th, 10th or 11th grade and who have earned at least a 3.3 GPA in their high school academic courses. Interested students should contact:

UCR Summer Sessions and Special Programs
1200 University Avenue
Riverside, CA 92507
Phone: (909) 787-3044
Web: http://summer.ucr.edu/

## University of Pennsylvania
### The Penn Summer Science Academy

Since 1987, more than a thousand high school students have explored careers in science, engineering, and mathematics through the Penn Summer Science Academy. PSSA, conducted by the College of General Studies at the University of Pennsylvania, is an intensive non-credit program consisting of both guided and independent laboratory projects, seminars, workshops, faculty lectures, discussion groups, and problem-solving sessions, all taught by Penn scientists and students.

The four-week program has grown from 28 to more than 150 students from all over the United States who choose a concentration in Molecular Biology, Materials Science, Environmental Science, Mathematics, or Physics. Students spend half their time in laboratory, fieldwork, or problem-solving sessions. They also take an innovative course called Issues in Science, in which they examine social, ethical, and legal issues related to the science they are learning. We assemble a 100-page book of excerpts from magazines, newspaper articles, and books, which form the basis for class discussions, role-playing sessions, debates, and written issue papers. Extensive use is also made of the many Web sites that deal with these issues.

Added to this is a class in computing and Internet skills. Each student receives an email account and access to the University's computing network. Carefully planned trips and occasional speakers round out the program. A full schedule of social activities, and access to Penn's gym and pool, keep students well occupied.

The PSSA is funded primarily by student fees. Grants from NSF and several corporations have provided financial aid for needy students.

Reach the PSSA at http://www.sas.upenn.edu/CGS/highschool/pssa.shtml

### University of Rochester

The program we have here for high school students is the Summer Science Academy. You can get all of the information you need on our web site: http://www.urmc.rochester.edu/smd/mbi/acad.html. This is a 4-week program for high school students who have taken biology. The program takes place at the Univ. of Rochester School of Medicine and Dentistry during July-August. The program offers hands-on lab activities in microbiology, molecular biology, immunology and environmental health topics. Also included are a bioethics course and a biocomputing course, as well as field trips and seminars by UR faculty. Tuition is currently $750 for the Summer 2000 program (July 10-August 4). A limited number of scholarships are available, based on financial need and academic merit. Hours of the program are Monday-Friday 9:30-3:00. Most of our students come from the greater Rochester area. Out of town students are placed with families of local students for housing. For more information, please contact:

Dina Markowitz, Ph.D.
Director, Community Outreach and Education Programs
University of Rochester
Environmental Health Sciences Center
575 Elmwood Avenue, Box EHSC
Rochester, NY 14642
716-275-3171
Fax: 716-256-2591

**Villanova University**
**Villanova-HHMI-NSF Summer Research Institute in Biology, Computing, and Mathematics**
Villanova University announces the third Summer Research Institute in Biology, Computing, and Mathematics for gifted high school students and high school teachers. The 2000 Summer Research Institute is funded by the National Science Foundation (NSF) under the new Teacher and Student Development Through Research Experiences Program and is part of science development and outreach activities funded by a 1996 Howard Hughes Medical Institute (HHMI) Undergraduate Biological Sciences Education Initiative Grant to Villanova.

Participants selected for the Villanova University-HHMI-NSF Summer Research Institute will investigate questions in one of three principal research areas: i) mathematical models in epidemiology and the population biology of the immune system; ii) ecology and ecosystem modeling; and iii) epidemiology of hypertension and other chronic diseases. Participants will work in teams composed of one teacher and three students. These research efforts will be built around the use of large-scale data collections including epidemiological data available through the Centers for Disease Control and publicly accessible sources of data on ecosystems and natural resources. Participants will work closely with program faculty from the Departments of Biology, Mathematical, and Computing Sciences at Villanova University and other institutions. Students of color and women are particularly encouraged to apply. For application forms, write or contact:

Professor William M. Fleischman
Villanova Summer Program in Biology, Computing & Mathematics
Department of Computing Sciences
Villanova University
Villanova, Pennsylvania 19085-1699
Phone: (610) 519-6018 email: biomath@villanova.edu
Web: http://www.csc.vill.edu/~vsri/

## Conclusion

From examining the descriptions provided here, you will notice that summer programs come in a variety of forms. Some are free, and others require tuition. Those that are free are primarily funded by individuals, the government, or national organizations. The subject matter and lengths of programs also differ. Our advice is to decide what field you are interested in and how much time you will have available during your summer. This is by no means a comprehensive list of the summer programs being offered throughout the United States. If you would like to add your program to this list, please contact us.

# APPENDIX D

## Useful Websites

This appendix lists by category over 100 websites that you may find helpful for one reason or another. Due to the "dynamic nature" of the Internet, this list is subject to change. Our website www.AcceleratedMed.com will always have an updated list among other things. Surf on over to our site right now and see what we have to offer – you may be surprised!

## Admissions

http://bestpremed.hypermart.net/
Alex's Illicit Guide to Medical School Admissions – Advice on the process from a student

http://www.premedical.com/
Premedical.com – Provides information about getting into medical or dental school

http://www.bol.ucla.edu/~ericwang/
Premedical and Medical School Admissions Guide – Advice on the pre-med track

http://www.voicenet.com/~popare/pocanmed.html
Canuck Medical School Application Help Page – resource for Canadians

http://www.camv.com/sean/medical.html
Medical School Admissions Advisory Page

http://www.fastweb.com/
FastWeb—The source for scholarship information

# Interviews

http://medplaza.com/premed/index.php3
#1 Pre-med Advisor – Information about interviews and sample questions

http://interviewfeedback.com/
Interview Feed Back Page: Tell us about your medical school interviews!

# Tests and Test Prep

http://www.ets.org/
ETS – Education Testing Service

http://www.collegeboard.com/
The College Board

http://www.usmle.org/
USMLE—United States Medical Licensing Examination

http://www.nbme.org/
National Board of Medical Examiners

http://www.kaplan.com/
Kaplan Test Prep

http://www.review.com/
The Princeton Review

http://www.berkeley-review.com/
Berkeley Review – MCAT Preparation

http://www.scomm.net/~greg/med-ed/
The Medical Education page – written by a medical student

http://hometown.aol.com/MedLounge/index.html
Interactive Medical Student Lounge

http://www.s2smed.com/
Student to Student

http://www.ttuhsc.edu/success/
SuccessTypes Medical Education Page: Dedicated to Your Academic Success

http://www2.musc.edu/MED/PC-Student_folder/~andy/docs/
medschool.html
How I Got Into Medical School

## Organizations

http://www.aamc.org/
Association of American Medical Colleges

http://www.ama-assn.org/
American Medical Association

http://www.aacom.org/
American Association of Colleges of Osteopathic Medicine

http://www.aoa-net.org/
American Osteopathic Association

http://www.amsa.org/
American Medical Student Association (AMSA)

http://www.hon.ch/home.html
Health on the Net—Internet health association

http://crick.fmed.uniba.sk/ifmsa/IFMSA.html
International Federation of Medical Students' Associations

http://www.who.org/
World Health Organization

http://www.sund.ku.dk/wfme/
World Federation for Medical Education

## Government Sites

http://www.nih.gov/
National Institutes of Health

http://www.hhs.gov/
Department of Health and Human Services

http://www.nsf.gov/
National Science Foundation

http://navymedicine.med.navy.mil/
Bureau of Medicine and Surgery

http://www.nlm.nih.gov/
National Library of Medicine

http://www.cdc.gov/
Centers for Disease Control and Prevention

http://www.fda.gov/
US Food and Drug Administration

## For Medical Students

http://www.studentdoc.com/
Medical Student Resource Guide—Information on medical school courses and residency

http://www.medicalstudent.com/
Medicalstudent.com—Online library of medical information

http://mail.med.upenn.edu/~nofsinge/surgeon.htm
Future Surgeon's Guide to Medical School

http://upalumni.org/medschool/
Medical School Resources—Heart Failure: Diary of a Third Year Medical Student

## For Doctors

http://www.medzilla.com/
Medzilla—Health related employment opportunities

http://www.gretmar.com:80/webdoctor/home.html
WebDoctor—Internet medical resources for physicians

http://www.cmeweb.com/ cmeWEB—Resource for continuing medical education on the web

## Journals

http://jama.ama-assn.org/
JAMA—Journal of the American Medical Association

http://www.nejm.org/content/
NEJM—New England Journal of Medicine

http://medicine.nature.com/
Nature: Medicine

http://primarycare.medscape.com/ABFP/JABFP/public/
journal.JABFP.html
Journal of the American Board of Family Practice

http://www.pediatrics.org/
Pediatrics

http://her.oupjournals.org/
Health Education Research

## Software and Interactive Web Learning

http://www.nlm.nih.gov/research/visible/visible_human.html
The Visible Human Project—Representing detailed anatomical
structures

http://www.med.und.nodak.edu/depts/fpc/oldpage/pblm.htm
University of North Dakota—Problem based cases

http://www.webcom.com/~wooming/mededuc.html
Medical Education Software Home Page—Reviews of medical education software

ftp://ftp.ucl.ac.uk/pub/users/reaawww/programs/
University College London—Medical education software

http://medicus.marshall.edu/mainmenu.htm
Marshall University School of Medicine—The Interactive Patient

http://www.helix.com/
Healthcare Education Learning & Information Exchange—Online
medical education

http://www.bcm.tmc.edu/class2000/sims/HeartSounds.html
Heart Sounds—Simulates different types of heartbeats

http://www.muhealth.org/~shrp/rtwww/rcweb/docs/sounds.html
University of Missouri—Lung sounds

http://www.innerbody.com/htm/body.html
Human Anatomy Online

http://www.ama-assn.org/insight/gen_hlth/atlas/atlas.htm
Atlas of the Human Body

http://chrononet.hypermart.net/
ChronoNet—Online medical web project

## Medical Communities and Resources

http://www.webmd.com/
WebMD – Vast resources relating to health and medicine

http://www.fedprac.com/
Federal Practitioner Online—Clinical articles and commentary

http://www.medscape.com/
Medscape—Daily medical news and information

http://www.studentdoctor.com/
StudentDoctor Network – Pre-med and medical student online
community

http://www.harrisonsonline.com/
Harrison's Online—Online medical database

http://www.goaskalice.columbia.edu/index.html
Go ask Alice!—Health question and answer site

http://www.vh.org/
Virtual Hospital—Medical reference for patients and doctors

http://www.imc.gsm.com/
Integrated Medical Curriculum—Online medical tutorials and self-tests

http://www.stanford.edu/~epw/mem/faq/
Medical Education FAQ

http://www.gradschools.com/search.html?clicktrade=155507
Graduate School directory—List of graduate school programs

## Health Search Engines

http://www.hon.ch/MedHunt/
Medhunt

http://www.mwsearch.com/
Medical World Search

http://omni.ac.uk/
OMNI: Organizing Medical Networked Information—UK bio-medical resources

http://www.graylab.ac.uk/omd/
Online Medical Dictionary

http://www.healthfinder.gov/
Health news and issues

## Links to Links

http://www.geocities.com/CollegePark/2932/main.html
Aabena's Premed Page: Information For Premeds by a Premed—
Links to relevant pre-med sites

http://www.geocities.com/CollegePark/Union/8194/premed.html
Brad's Premed Resource Center—Many links divided by sections

http://www.webring.org/cgi-bin/webring?ring=mededrg&list
Medical Education Ring

http://www.lib.uiowa.edu/hardin/md/
Hardin Meta Directory—Lists sites from each specialty

http://webber.uib.no/isf/guide/edu.htm
Primary Care Internet Guide—Lists medical newsgroups, societies, and journals

http://www.medsite.com/
Medsite—Search tools for physicians

http://www.medicalstudent.net/index.html
Medicalstudent.net—Links to buy MCAT and medical school books

## Medical Schools and Universities with Accelerated or Combined Degree Programs (alphabetically)

http://www.bcm.tmc.edu/
Baylor College of Medicine

http://www.binghamton.edu/
Binghamton University

http://web.bu.edu/
Boston University

http://www.brooklyn.cuny.edu/
Brooklyn College

http://www.brown.edu/
Brown University

http://www.cwru.edu/
Case Western Reserve University

http://www.finchcms.edu/cms/medschool.html
Chicago Medical School

http://www.tcnj.edu/
The College of New Jersey

http://www.wm.edu/
The College of William and Mary

http://www.drew.edu/
Drew University

http://www.evms.edu/
Eastern Virginia Medical School

http://www.etsu-tn.edu/
East Tennessee State University

http://www.fisk.edu/
Fisk University

http://www.gwumc.edu/
George Washington University School of Medicine

http://www.howard.edu/
Howard University

http://www.iit.edu/
Illinois Institute of Technology

http://www.tju.edu/
Jefferson Medical College

http://www.kent.edu/
Kent State University

http://www.lehigh.edu
Lehigh University

http://www.lsumc.edu/
Louisiana State University of Health Sciences

http://www.auhs.edu/
MCP Hahnemann University

http://www.chm.msu.edu/
Michigan State University

http://www.montclair.edu/
Montclair State University

http://www.njit.edu/
New Jersey Institute of Technology

http://www.nyu.edu/
New York University

http://www.nsu.edu/
Norfolk State University

http://www.neoucom.edu/
Northeastern Ohio Universities College of Medicine

http://www.nums.nwu.edu/
Northwestern University Medical School

http://www.odu.edu/
Old Dominion University

http://www.psu.edu/
Pennsylvania State University

http://www.rpi.edu/
Rensselaer Polytechnic Institute

http://www.rice.edu/
Rice University

http://www2.stockton.edu/
Richard Stockton College of New Jersey

http://www.rutgers.edu/
Rutgers University

http://www.siena.edu/
Siena College

http://www.stevens-tech.edu/
Stevens Institute of Technology

http://www.hscbklyn.edu/
SUNY—Brooklyn College of Medicine

http://www.union.edu/
Union College

http://www.uakron.edu/
University of Akron

http://main.uab.edu/uasom/
University of Alabama School of Medicine

http://www.medsch.ucla.edu/
UCLA School of Medicine

http://www.umdnj.edu/
UMDNJ—New Jersey Medical School

http://www.miami.edu/
University of Miami

http://www.umich.edu/
University of Michigan

http://www.umkc.edu/
University of Missouri

http://www.rochester.edu/
University of Rochester

http://www.usouthal.edu/
University of South Alabama

http://www.usc.edu/
University of Southern California

http://www.biostat.wisc.edu/
University of Wisconsin Medical School

http://www.vill.edu/
Villanova University

http://www.ysu.edu/
Youngstown State University

# CONTACT INFO

If you have any additional questions about the process, do not hesitate in contacting us. We'd love to hear from you. If you have any ideas, suggestions or contributions (anecdotal or informative), please send them as well. We'd especially be interested in your personal advice to accelerated program hopefuls and unexpected success stories of how you did something great, despite adversity. You just may find yourself as a contributor in our next edition. Finally, feel free to contact us about presenting at schools, etc., or any business aspects relating to this book or future projects involving our expertise. If you just want to send an e-mail to say hi, that's OK too!

Ashish Raju
224-26 77th Avenue
Bayside, NY 11364
AshishRaju@yahoo.com

Jason Yanofski
10 Gavin Road
West Orange, NJ 07052
AcceleratedMed@aol.com

Visit our web page at www.AcceleratedMed.com for more information, news, and resources. The web site will also provide instructions to order additional copies of *From High School to Med. School.*

# ABOUT THE AUTHORS

**Ashish Raju** was born in India on July 22, 1980. He came to the United States at age two where he later became a citizen. He attended Benjamin N. Cardozo High School in Bayside, New York and graduated valedictorian in a class of over 800 students. He has appeared in several forms of media from CNN to *Newsday*. He is a National Merit Scholar, Advanced Placement Scholar, and Brown University Book Award recipient. While in high school, he received numerous awards and accolades that include the Bausch & Lomb Honorary Science Medal and James Hacket Award in Oratory. In 1998, Ashish and his team won the New York City Chase Bank Lincoln Douglas Debates by defeating all other public schools in the city.

While in high school, Ashish was involved in several clubs. He was captain and coach of the speech and debate team, editor of the science paper, and member of Arista honors society. After turning down several Ivy League schools, he attended Lehigh University's six-year BA/MD program to pursue a career in medicine. At Lehigh, he has continued to maintain an active role on campus. Ashish is a Dean's scholar, president of his dorm, peer tutor, executive member of the Indian Students Association, tour guide, and member of Alpha Phi Omega fraternity and Phi Eta Sigma Honors Society. He also has learned how to play the tabla and classical Indian dance for over four years.

Colleagues and friends describe Ashish as a true "renaissance" man. From dancing to research, he is a truly dynamic individual. After completing his studies at Lehigh this year, he will be attending MCP Hahnemann Medical School in the fall.

**Jason Russell Yanofski** was born in New York on May 21, 1980. He graduated from West Orange High School in West Orange, New Jersey in 1998 at the top of his class. During high school he was active as a volunteer Emergency Medical Technician for the West Orange First Aid Squad, aiding his community. He also served as Youth Squad Captain recruiting, training, and leading the rest of the team. Jason participated in scientific research through Rutgers University, helping to genetically determine the phylogenetic tree of the onion. He was active in the National Honor Society and as a captain on the wrestling team. He also took advanced college courses at night, as well as receiving countless academic awards. Jason also worked as a computer consultant and technician for companies as a personal agent.

Jason was accepted into a combined 6-year BA/MD accelerated medical program through Lehigh University in affiliation with MCP Hahnemann University. Impressively, he was able to pass his Medical College Admissions Test requirement the summer before matriculation to college, just after his eighteenth birthday. At Lehigh, Jason was a Dean's scholar and was known as an active student on campus. He was a brother of Sigma Alpha Mu fraternity (being the first student in the history of the combined program at Lehigh to pledge) and served as scholarship chair.

Jason is creative, ambitious, and has an unparalleled sense of humor. Everyone who knows him agrees that there is no doubt his ingenuity will take him far in life, within the medical field and outside of it. This book is his first major literary project, and he hopes it will change the lives of his readers.

Printed in the United States
76983LV00002B/33